ECONOMIC RESEARCH CENTRE

REPORT OF THE
NINETY-SEVENTH ROUND TABLE
ON TRANSPORT ECONOMICS

held in Paris on 4th-5th November 1993
on the following topic:

CHARGING FOR THE USE OF URBAN ROADS

EUROPEAN CONFERENCE OF MINISTERS OF TRANSPORT

THE EUROPEAN CONFERENCE
OF MINISTERS OF TRANSPORT (ECMT)

The European Conference of Ministers of Transport (ECMT) is an inter-governmental organisation established by a Protocol signed in Brussels on 17th October 1953. The Council of the Conference comprises the Ministers of Transport of 31 European countries.[1] The work of the Council of Ministers is prepared by a Committee of Deputies.

The purposes of the Conference are:

   a) to take whatever measures may be necessary to achieve, at general or regional level, the most efficient use and rational development of European inland transport of international importance;

   b) to co-ordinate and promote the activities of international organisations concerned with European inland transport, taking into account the work of supranational authorities in this field.

The matters generally studied by ECMT – and on which the Ministers take decisions – include: the general lines of transport policy; investment in the sector; infrastructural needs; specific aspects of the development of rail, road and inland waterways transport; combined transport issues; urban travel; road safety and traffic rules, signs and signals; access to transport for people with mobility problems. Other subjects now being examined in depth are: the future applications of new technologies, protection of the environment, and the integration of the Central and Eastern European countries in the European transport market. Statistical analyses of trends in traffic and investment are published each year, thus throwing light on the prevailing economic situation.

The ECMT organises Round Tables and Symposia. Their conclusions are considered by the competent organs of the Conference, under the authority of the Committee of Deputies, so that the latter may formulate proposals for policy decisions to be submitted to the Ministers.

The ECMT Documentation Centre maintains the TRANSDOC database, which can be accessed on-line via the telecommunications network.

For administrative purposes, the ECMT Secretariat is attached to the Secretariat of the Organisation for Economic Co-operation and Development (OECD).

1. Austria, Belgium, Bosnia-Herzegovina, Bulgaria, Croatia, the Czech Republic, Denmark, Estonia, Finland, France, Germany, Greece, Hungary, Ireland, Italy, Latvia, Lithuania, Luxembourg, Moldova, the Netherlands, Norway, Poland, Portugal, Romania, the Slovak Republic, Slovenia, Spain, Sweden, Switzerland, Turkey and the United Kingdom. (Associate Member countries: Australia, Canada, Japan, New Zealand, the Russian Federation and the United States. Observer countries: Albania, Morocco.)

Publié en français sous le titre :
LES PÉAGES ROUTIERS URBAINS
TABLE RONDE 97

TABLE OF CONTENTS

NORWAY

A. HERVIK
Molde College

S. BRAATHEN
Møreforsking Molde
Molde
Norway

SUMMARY

Molde, June 1993

1. INTRODUCTION

In economic price theory we find a long tradition of how social efficiency concerning charging of urban infrastructure can be developed. Efficient use of urban infrastructure should be encouraged through prices based on social marginal costs. In theory, the characteristics of both optimum charging systems and optimum infrastructure systems within transportation are formally quite similar to the characteristics of long- and short- run equilibrium in the purely competitive industries. It is important to underline the importance of economic rationality in charging systems and the analytical framework that we find in Mohring (1976), a textbook with a microeconomic market perspective on traffic in urban areas. The simple market perspective is often lost in more detailed traffic planning and modelling and so are also the fundamental economic theories on charging systems and investment criteria. The chart we use is simple but covers the main aspects. We will also discuss the new and more complex "structural model of peak period congestion" (Small, 1992).

This paper will not focus on the theoretical aspects. Even though we are looking at charging systems from a practical point of view, it will be important to distinguish between short-term and long-term marginal costs. There is a close connection between charging systems both in the short run focusing on income and short-term marginal costs, and in the long run with incentives to increase capacity, investment criteria and long-run marginal costs.

The main objectives to be met by any charging system are:

-- Promote efficient use of the infrastructure;
-- Generate financing to expand capacity to satisfy user needs;
-- Promote an efficient environmental policy;
-- Provide designs which are acceptable politically and by the public at large.

Users should be charged according to their willingness to pay the real cost of offering the infrastructure (including external costs). In practice, these

9

theoretical guidelines have proved difficult to follow. The charging system that will be implemented in most countries will be based on second best pricing. Charging systems for urban infrastructure will not only concentrate on efficiency criteria but will focus extensively on the need for financial support to implement expansive political infrastructure programmes. Trade-offs between the need for financial support and the efficiency criteria might become an important issue in the near future.

Under the following assumptions (and if we define urban infrastructures as a local collective good) general theory points out that the efficient charging system is general taxation with a public sector responsibility:

--   If existing infrastructure can be used by everyone without influencing other users (no external effects and excess capacity);
--   If the cost structure defines the infrastructure as a natural monopoly with declining average cost and very low marginal costs;
--   If the infrastructure cannot easily be divided and sold as individual goods.

If all these assumptions are fulfilled, urban infrastructure should be financed by general taxation and the public sector should be responsible for supplying these goods. The price for users should be close to zero and the charging systems will be defined as a general taxation problem.

As we all know, these three main assumptions will all prove to be wrong. This is partly the reason why the charging systems for the infrastructure are in focus, both in the "scientific world" and, more practically, to finance the costly infrastructure development programmes in most countries in Europe. The trend in developing tax systems is moving towards simpler systems with less weight on direct tax on labour, but also towards more indirect taxation where the tax system is designed with intent to correct market imperfections. Taxation on fuel will be simple and cheap to collect. It will give incentives to internalise costs and external effects connected to the use of infrastructure. The main elements concerning infrastructure charging systems can be summarised as follows:

--   Fuel taxation should as an average be able to finance the long-term marginal costs connected to use of urban infrastructure. This will give users the right incentives to reflect willingness to pay for the total long term marginal costs;
--   As the cost structure will vary a great deal, the taxation should be differentiated between different regions and cities. This will imply large practical problems because long distance travellers will not pay taxes

where they use the infrastructure. In addition, there may be incentives to refuel where it is cheapest (outside the area), and other charging systems like tolls or parking fees will have to be implemented;

-- "Road pricing" will be the "perfect" charging system to correct for the regional differences (external effects and differences in long-term marginal costs) that petrol taxation will not be able to handle;

-- Tolls or toll rings can be the "second best" charging systems for urban infrastructure. There is now a widespread use of such systems in different countries in combination with fuel taxation.

In the long run, we can expect a road pricing charging system (*Corporation of London*, 1990):

"We have no doubt that *in the long term the introduction of some form of road pricing will be essential to achieve efficient management and development of London's transport. This should not be contemplated until sufficient capacity increases in the rail network are in place, so that users have a genuine choice of mode.* It is important in the meantime to address the practical issues of implementation.

Experience from several other countries, as well as our consultations in London in the course of this exercise, suggests that *objections to road pricing would be significantly reduced and perhaps even eliminated if there were some guarantee that the revenues would be ploughed back into the system.* In Britain, there is a general though not overriding predisposition to avoid earmarking of taxes or other revenues on the understandable grounds that this can introduce unwarranted rigidities into expenditure allocation. We feel sure that any difficulties on this score would be allayed by ensuring regular reviews of the purposes and structure of the earmarking arrangement."

Even if the technology is available and continuously improving with respect to electronic road pricing systems, there is reason to believe that it will take some time before the system will be implemented in full scale. Jones and Hervik (1992) discuss the trends in the use of road pricing and barriers to introducing such charging systems. In the meantime, a combination of fuel taxation and toll rings/toll stations (and licensing) on certain links will be the challenge.

Several countries try to decide on petrol taxation equal to the long-run marginal costs as a principle for an efficient infrastructure charging system. This is not at all convenient as a principle in other countries where fuel taxation is very controversial politically. In Norway, we try to connect the fuel taxation debate to this principle. The latest calculations indicate that the fuel tax is too high compared to long-run marginal costs (but most people and politicians still hold the opinion that the fuel tax is too low when we also take CO_2 emissions into consideration). In addition to fuel taxes, Norway also has toll rings around the three largest cities (Oslo, Bergen and Trondheim). There is an extra toll station for financing a special main road leading into town (with very high tariffs in Bergen, medium-sized in Trondheim and quite low in Oslo). Several toll roads lead into smaller towns where the charging system is established to finance a new bridge or a sub-sea tunnel. Norway now has a total of 20 urban infrastructure charging systems in function (toll rings counted as one). Several ferries serve towns where the commuters pay for the use of this urban infrastructure. One city (Tromsø) implemented a local fuel tax to finance new infrastructure instead of a toll ring. The reason was that this gave much lower collection costs. The city lies far north in an area with modest possibilities of extensive refuelling outside town.

Norway is thus a small laboratory for studying the effects from different charging systems. Only the introduction of toll roads in Randstadt in the Netherlands is similar to this system, even though we have numerous examples of toll roads to finance new bridges leading into town centres in other countries (but compared in size this occurs on a smaller scale both in France and Italy). In the near future, we may see a growth in toll roads because road building may become a central measure against unemployment, based on the belief that this measure can stimulate economic growth. Private financing is chosen because of tight public budgets.

In this paper we will concentrate on microeconomic aspects, and we will not discuss if the policy described will be an efficient economic policy to achieve the objectives in a macroeconomic perspective. Since most countries have unbalanced public budgets they will not be able to afford these infrastructure programmes without public payment through toll stations or increased petrol taxation (in many countries more controversial than toll roads). A main question is the trade-offs between collection costs (operating costs of the collection system, time costs and inconvenience costs brought upon motorists) in toll systems and allocation costs and political controversies connected to increased fuel tax.

This leads into another main aspect connected to the decision problem in introducing toll roads. All toll rings in Norway were introduced as a part of building new infrastructure, and all income from tolls is earmarked for investment in new infrastructure in the region (roads and/or public transport). This question

12

of earmarking is an important issue in the decision process. In many countries this is a difficult matter and, as in Norway, it will imply law changes.

Another aspect is the more detailed design of the charging system. The discount system is very important as far as political and public acceptance is concerned. All systems in Norway started with quite significant discounts for frequent users. This is done in different ways on different toll roads. Some have time-limited cards (month/year), i.e. not individual payment for each trip. Most places now have electronic systems that can differentiate the discount for users according to travel frequency. Considering probability of political acceptance, it seems to be important to take the frequent travellers into consideration by introducing discounts. This is not at all rational considering social efficiency and not even regarding distributive effects. It is still not accepted that frequent users should be charged too much, because of their dependence on use. The experience of market reactions to discount systems is that discounts often lead to strong adaption to the discount system, a large increase in the number of discount users and revenue loss.

A third aspect concerns the distribution of planning responsibility between local and central authorities regarding infrastructure. Fuel taxation will, in most countries, be the responsibility of the central authorities. Toll rings and toll roads will, in most cases, be the responsibility of local authorities. This introduces an incentive problem. Why finance infrastructure by local toll payment when you have already paid for the long-term marginal cost of infrastructure through fuel taxation? The relations between decisions made by local and central authorities can introduce game situations with incentive problems such as: Why increase toll fares to finance new infrastructure if you can get "common pool" money from central authorities allocated to road building? The common pool problem is well known in theory and one practical (and theoretical) piece of advice is to provide one dollar from central authorities to each dollar you collect locally to finance new infrastructure. This sharing of costs is now in practice in the Norwegian system. Toll rings are a quite new phenomenon, and we have no real experience of change in strategic behaviour in the relations between central and local authorities.

In this paper we will discuss four main points:

-- The theoretical and practical problems of charging systems through fuel taxation paying for use of urban infrastructure. We will consider fuel taxation as an indirect user charge.

-- Toll roads/toll rings (and other direct charging systems such as licensing for the use of land and parking fees) as an alternative charging system or a supplementary charging system to petrol taxation.
-- The more theoretically satisfactory system "road pricing" as an alternative to this more "second best" situation which combines petrol tax and toll roads/toll rings.
-- (Briefly) Charging systems for public urban infrastructures such as train, light train and bus services.

2. PETROL TAXATION AS A CHARGING SYSTEM FOR URBAN INFRASTRUCTURE

Petrol taxation can be considered as a charging system for the urban infrastructure. Most European countries have petrol taxation at a level that generates heavy total income. In many countries these taxes generate a higher annual income than the yearly expenditure in maintaining and investing in roads. Petrol taxation is a charging system for the use of roads, and users pay a tax that will influence their economic incentives for car use. Since this petrol tax is not paid for individual trips, we call this tax an indirect charging system for the use of infrastructure. In most European countries this will be the most important infrastructure charging system. It is an open question whether charges of marginal costs through petrol taxation give weaker incentives to regulate traffic than direct charging systems (tolls and parking fees). Estimations of price elasticity indicate that tolls cause a more direct reaction in the market ($e_{ii} = -0.5$), while short-run elasticity on fuel is lower ($e_{ii} = -0.3$). The long run effects might give more equal elasticities (Goodwin and Jones, 1989). Experience from Norwegian toll roads indicate that elasticities on tolls in the short run can be even lower than -0.5 (Hervik, *et al.* 1992). Table 1 gives an overview of the different categories of charging systems.

The user fees urban motorists face are two-component fees consisting of both fixed and variable charges. The fixed fees are generally in the form of acquisition charges (sales taxes on new vehicles), annual registration fees and driving licence fees. The most common forms of variable charges are motor fuel taxes, weight-distance charges for trucks and parking fees. In addition, many areas make use of toll rings/toll roads around urban areas. Some have made use of other use-variable fees such as supplementary licensing.

14

An important aspect of this issue is whether this is a part of the general taxation system and motivated by fiscal reasons only, or if these charging systems are designed from the need to regulate the use of the infrastructure. The main elements in the general taxation system imposed on vehicles consist of:

-- Sales taxes;
-- Annual registration fee;
-- Fuel taxes.

The total tax level on motorists will influence the car use and in a wider sense (in the long run) sales taxes can be considered as a charging system for the use of the infrastructure. We will in this chapter consider both sales taxation and the annual registration fee as mostly motivated by fiscal reasons. We will return to the annual registration fee more from the viewpoint that this can be differentiated in space and time. This fee can be expanded to an area licence system that is a charging system for use of urban infrastructure (as in Singapore). In general, this annual registration fee can be interpreted as a fixed charge for access to the road. This interpretation makes the annual registration fee a part of a two-tariff charging system for the use of infrastructure. The most common way to treat this annual registration fee is as a tax motivated by fiscal reasons only. This chapter will concentrate on fuel taxes.

When we consider fuel tax as a charging system for the use of infrastructure, this does not imply that this tax should be earmarked for infrastructure development. It does, however, imply that this tax gives an economic rationality for analysing whether the total income through this user tax is sufficient to cover total infrastructure costs. Analyses carried out in accordance with transportation economics textbooks will conclude that fuel tax should, in principle, pay the total marginal cost, both infrastructure costs and external effects (if we have no other charging systems for the use). One main theoretical principle states that if external effects are not included, the yearly income from petrol taxation should cover the total infrastructure costs (investment and maintenance costs). From this conclusion, it is very easy to go a little bit further and say that petrol tax should be earmarked to cover infrastructure costs. This is not an accepted principle in the general tax debate. There are no reasons (except maybe political reasons) to connect this income and cost aspect directly to each other. From an efficiency point of view, total income from petrol taxation should not deviate too much from total infrastructure costs (no tolls and no corrections for external costs like environmental costs). If fuel taxation gives a much higher income this could either be motivated by corrections for external costs or by fiscal reasons (fuel is an efficient commodity for taxation because the allocation loss is small with low demand elasticity compared to other commodities).

15

Let us first look at the optimal fuel tax from a theoretical perspective before we turn to the more practical problems of implementing economically optimal petrol taxation. Figure 1 presents the traditional theoretical chart to analyse short-term marginal costs and optimal charging systems for urban infrastructure. The more detailed theoretical discussion can be found in Mohring (1976). The presentation is based on infrastructure with a given capacity and a given connection between increasing traffic and increasing average and marginal travel time. With an optimal fuel tax, the marginal user will pay the total short-term capacity cost, that will be equal here to the external congestion costs. In this optimum we will have a charging system where the users cover the short-term marginal costs. In this sense this will be an optimal charging system for the use of this urban infrastructure.

Setting the charging system equal to the marginal cost for highway trips is not necessarily incompatible with a self-supporting system. Given constant returns to scale there will be two simple rules that will lead to both short-term rationality for the use of existing infrastructure and to long-run optimum network capacity:

-- Establishing short-run marginal cost prices for the use of each link in an existing infrastructure by, for example, petrol taxation to correct the difference between the short-run marginal costs and the average variable costs of trips.
-- Changing the size of each link to the point where the revenue from fuel taxation covers the exact costs to the authorities of providing that link, including maintenance and other operating costs, depreciation and capital costs.

This simple figure and those two rules give the main guidelines for the optimal charging systems for urban infrastructure. The charging system through petrol taxation should cover the short-term marginal capacity costs (the difference between the short-run marginal and short-run average cost curve) and these costs should be equal to the long-run capacity costs. This implies that no increased investment should take place before the willingness to pay in the short-run also covers the long-term marginal costs (the capacity costs). But this will also imply that in the optimal situation (as an average) the income from the total petrol tax should also exactly cover the total infrastructure costs.

It follows that an average petrol taxation system should cover infrastructure costs for the average system. But this average system is not very easy to implement. First of all we will have large differences between different regions, between different times of the day and between cars and trucks. In urban areas the opportunity costs of land will be much higher than in rural areas and therefore long-term marginal costs will be different. Secondly, the congestion costs will differ very much between areas and especially through different times of the day. During morning and evening peaks short-term capacity costs will be much higher in urban areas than in rural areas and in off-peak hours. Trucks may also impose much higher short-term marginal costs on infrastructure use than their contribution through fuel taxation. It will not be possible to differentiate fuel tax between regions and time of the day to take these fundamental differences into consideration. Only a very technically advanced road pricing system will enable us to solve this problem by differentiating electronic payment according to differences in short-term marginal costs for different links. We will return to toll systems and road pricing in a later chapter.

Fuel taxation should be a user charge for the average infrastructure system. What is an average system? We will have to exclude the urban areas, and especially the peak hours from an average system. The short-term marginal costs will be very high here, and there will be no rationality in implementing a fuel tax that will charge these high marginal costs in off-peak hours. Such an undifferentiated charging system will imply too high taxes, and the system will not give a rational signal on infrastructure costs to the users in other regions and outside peak hours. Charging too much will cause a rationing of demand for transport where willingness to pay actually covers the short-run marginal costs. This will imply a misallocation of resources.

As a basis for the Norwegian political petrol tax debate we calculated the short- and long-term marginal costs. The empirical model has many uncertainties. It is based on historical data. This implies that the certain historical period in question must be representative for the future and that investments have actually increased capacity in an optimal way historically to give "correct" empirical figures. It is also an empirical problem that the estimation depends on the specific period used for estimating the model. The calculation is based on the capacity investments in that period. All maintenance costs connected to this investment are added. The cost responsibility is also shared between cars and trucks in a cost sharing model. These cost figures are connected to increased traffic for the same period to establish the long-term marginal cost. The costs connected to infrastructure with congestion problems are excluded (urban areas). Long-term marginal costs are corrected for inflation and we end up with a figure giving us an indication of long-run marginal costs and the optimal petrol tax level for infrastructure with low congestion costs.

This calculation has many assumptions and uncertainties, but it still gives an indication of a charging system with incentives for efficient use of infrastructure outside congested areas. The tax level in Norway is somewhat higher than ECU 0.5 per litre. The conclusion from this calculation (NOU 1992:3) is that cars already cover their cost responsibility including a CO_2 tax (the CO_2 tax is ECU 0.1 per litre, higher than in most European countries). The most uncertain part of this calculation will be (as pointed out by Newbery, 1988) the calculation of accident costs. These might be wrong with a factor of 10. In the Norwegian calculation we used the simple cost model of what accidents will cost in terms of lost production and increase in public service costs, but excluding willingness to pay for avoiding accidents. Newbery also stresses the problem of congestion and value of time as uncertain factors. We will return to these aspects in the next chapter. For trucks, the clear conclusion is that they do not pay their full cost responsibility. In total, the income from petrol taxation covers the infrastructure costs in Norway, both maintenance and investment costs. In addition, there are toll rings and toll roads in urban areas with congestion that give a revenue of more than 25 per cent of the total fuel tax income. Table 2 shows the share of indirect user charges in selected European countries compared to total expenditure on road investments. Fuel taxation gives a revenue of 4 times as much as vehicle taxation on an average. Tolls count for less than 0.5 per cent of the total revenue. Only France and Italy have a revenue from tolls of 10-15 per cent. The revenue is 25 per cent higher than the expenditure on roads as an average. In Norway, this figure is approximately 50 per cent. In most countries this gap between revenue and expenditure is motivated by the objective to discourage energy consumption and associated emissions. There is a general political trend to try to expand this gap because of these overall objectives. Internationally the environmental movement also focuses on fuel tax. Accident costs are used here as an argument for increase (*The European Federation for Transport and Environment*). There is a need for a consensus debate in calculation of accident costs to avoid the strong discrepancies in calculations on optimal fuel taxation.

Table 3 shows the differences in fuel taxes between different countries. There are still great differences between countries. The EC "target" fuel tax is on the upper limit ECU 0.5/litre (in Norway, Italy and Denmark). European taxes are much higher than in the USA. In Europe, there is also a common understanding that trucks pay a relatively smaller share for their use of infrastructure, creating competitive distortion against rail freight. In Europe, it is not common to differentiate the fuel tax within countries, e.g. between urban and rural areas. In the USA, there are many states that have higher fuel taxes than the federal taxation.

In 1990, a special regional extra fuel tax was introduced to finance new infrastructure in the Tromsø area. This was possible in this area because the distances to the nearest competing petrol stations are quite far. The extra tax was set at less than 10 per cent of the petrol price. The experiences so far have been positive in giving financial support to new road building. The price elasticity seems to have been very small (less than - 0.2), but there has been a decrease in the sales of petrol because people have been motivated to refuel outside Tromsø when travelling in other districts. It has not been possible to discover any interregional travelling just for refuelling. Collection costs connected to this local petrol tax are much cheaper than for tolls (as will be discussed in the next chapter).

Differentiated petrol tax in urban areas to finance the extra infrastructure costs in such areas can be a charging system worth trying in some regions. In the USA, many states have extra fuel tax (OECD 1985). This will, of course, generate some refuelling in other regions, but most of the refuelling or use of urban infrastructure is done by locals, and will take place within the fuel tax area. Norway has decided not to go any further than this experiment in Tromsø. The introduction of a system like this must involve earmarking of the local tax. A differentiation is not at all the optimal solution. It may still be an alternative in some areas where no other solutions are politically acceptable.

Regional differences in the annual registration tax can be another regional user charge to finance new infrastructure. This could be an alternative where you avoid the problem of refuelling in other regions. This will give no user incentives because one does not pay for use. A problem with "free riders" who do not live in the "high charge" area but frequently use its infrastructure will occur. An efficiency perspective will imply that it is correct that people in rural regions pay less for use through lower annual fees when there are no capacity limits and no need for incentives to ration the use of infrastructure. On the other hand, it is not efficient that people in urban areas pay a high charge for having a car if they do not use it in peak hours.

3. TOLL ROADS, TOLL RINGS, LICENSING AND PARKING FEES AS CHARGING SYSTEMS FOR THE USE OF INFRASTRUCTURE

Figure 2 illustrates some main reasons why direct charging through tolls is a more efficient way to pay for the use of infrastructure. The figure is similar to Figure 1, only it shows that optimal tolls can vary a great deal between different market segments. A1-B1 shows the optimal charge when demand is low and there is not too much congestion (outside peak hours or in rural areas). The optimal toll will be much lower than A2-B2 which shows optimal toll for infrastructure with high marginal short-term congestion costs. As discussed in the previous chapter, this illustrates the weakness of using fuel tax as a charging system. This charging system will have to charge an average price for short-term capacity costs and this kind of average charging will mean allocation losses. The cross-hatched areas in Figure 2 show the allocation loss by charging too much outside peak hours when traffic will be too low (X_1) compared to optimal traffic (X_2). In peak hours charges will be too low and give too much traffic (X_4) compared to the optimum (X_3). If the price elasticity is very inelastic allocation losses will also be low and it does not matter too much what kind of charging system is used.

It will not be possible to differentiate the fuel prices between peak and off-peak hours and between different links with and without high short-term marginal costs. This will be for the benefit of toll roads or toll rings. Motorists can be directly charged for the use of infrastructure with capacity limits and easily differentiated in time according to peak hours. On certain links it will, in theory, be easy to charge the short-term marginal costs as illustrated in Figure 2. This has been done on 20 urban infrastructure links in Norway. Around all the largest cities we have toll rings, and one has to pay to enter the inner towns of Oslo, Bergen and Trondheim. The total income from tolls in Norway equals 25 per cent of the income from fuel tax.

The principles of the toll system illustrated in Figure 2 give us the main perspective of why tolls should be used as a supplement to indirect charging through fuel tax. Tolls could be levied on certain roads with congestion and could be differentiated to certain days or times of day when the external costs are very high. One main obstacle why this charging system is not implemented in European cities is that it is not very easy to set up tolls on all roads. Setting up tolls on the main roads will give incentives to shift to non-tolled routes which may be less safe and have a higher (local) environmental impact. Even though it is easy to argue that the route structure and incentives to choose different routes are so complicated that it is not easy to predict all the impacts of introducing tolls in large European cities, the technology of electronic charging systems is developing so rapidly that we now have systems that can compensate for these allocation/planning problems. It is possible to have toll stations on all main roads leading into town centres with optoelectronic recognition and data processing. Most cars will not have to stop to pay the charge. To avoid the problem of choosing other routes, electronic recognition with tolls can be implemented on these routes to regulate traffic. The level put on tolls can be chosen by experience in a sort of "stepwise refinement". Technological flexibility makes it possible to achieve the main goals in traffic regulation through the charging systems. The general price level, routes that will be charged, differentiation of charges for different times of day and routes will give the necessary tool to develop the charging system based on experience of how the market responds to the design of the charging system. It is, however, not possible to give advance calculations of optimum charges.

It is possible to establish some kind of understanding and experience of how to give a reasonable introductory charging system. The reasons for not implementing this charging system are mainly political. People show inertia to leave a well-known system (traffic jam and long travel time). This is based on an underlying fear that tolls will be just another general tax that will not give any value for money (less traffic jam and improved infrastructure service).

From the experience in Norway, where we have toll rings around all our major cities, we will begin with the experience from the political decision process. The responsibility for introducing tolls was delegated to the local authorities level. For local authorities the main motivation was that through tolls they could shorten by 50 per cent the period to reach a high standard infrastructure. It was necessary to make law changes to earmark the income from tolls for use on expenditure on roads and public transport infrastructure in the area where it was collected. It was also necessary to establish an incentive system of sharing costs between local and central authorities leading to a 50/50 model where each dollar made available by toll released another from central authorities. It was also necessary to introduce a discount for frequent travellers to avoid giving them a too heavy economic burden.

Despite this, there was major resistance among people in the influence area against the introduction of tolls. Surveys showed that politicians acted against majority. That was one reason why central authorities, especially in Oslo, had to "push" on the local decision process. The system was nearly not introduced at all. The equity problem arises especially in Oslo because it is not possible to locate the toll stations around the centre so all travels will be charged. Since some areas will always be uncharged, people who live in a similar region with toll charges will recognise this as unfair. It is important to locate the toll stations so as to minimise conflicts between people living in different areas. This can create a conflict concerning the most efficient location of the toll stations.

The experience both in Oslo and Bergen from surveys after opening was that the opinion very soon changed to being very positive to the charging system. In Oslo, one main reason could have been that the opening of the charging system took place at the same time as the opening of a new tunnel leading traffic underground through the town centre. Traffic jams in peak hours declined significantly. Norwegian cities have a less complicated structure than large

European cities. It is therefore much easier to introduce a toll system without large problems with people choosing alternative, uncharged routes. It is possible to charge almost all roads leading into the centre of town.

What is the economic experience so far? The first problem is that the collection costs in Norwegian toll rings are much higher (15-20 per cent of total income) than the indirect charging system. The second problem is that it is not politically easy to use the electronic charging system to differentiate between times of day and to regulate traffic.

In Oslo, a monthly and annual card system was established not paying for individual trips. The motivation for this was to prevent too many cars from stopping to pay, especially during peak hours. These time-limited cards were introduced because the electronic system was not established when the toll stations opened. After the introduction of electronic charging it has not been politically easy to skip annual cards and introduce individual charging systems with discounts to frequent travellers. The discount of the annual cards has been significant. This has resulted in a large segment travelling with annual cards.

Toll rings in Norway have proved to be an efficient mechanism for financing new infrastructure. In Oslo, Bergen and Trondheim the income has been close to the budget and is now at the level of close to NKr 1 billion yearly. This counts for approximately 13 per cent of total road investment in Norway and covers half the investment costs in these cities.

The experience with the electronic charging systems has proved to be very positive. There is modest cheating and the systems seem to be quite safe. In Oslo, 60 per cent now use the electronic system for paying while this share is 80 per cent in Trondheim. No problems with delays because of the toll stations have been reported.

The traffic in peak hours has not changed very much because of these tolls. The main reason is the price level and especially the discount system. The discounts are approximately one ECU per passage as an average for those with an annual card in Oslo (a little less in Bergen). Since there is no real discrimination during peak hours to pay the high marginal capacity costs, there has not been any decrease in traffic during peak hours because of tolls. In total, the traffic level is reduced by 5-6 per cent, but this is mainly off-peak travelling. In Trondheim, they have introduced a charging system with somewhat higher peak hour charges. The differentiation is too low to give incentives to changes in peak hour travelling. In Oslo, research has shown that peak hour charges should be four times today's differences between optimal tolls in peak and off-peak hours. There are cases where the difference counts a factor of 10 (Small, 1992). In Bergen and Trondheim, there is no charge at weekends and during nights. This proves correct according to the price theory because short-term marginal costs (capacity costs) will be low in these periods.

In most decisions in Norway charging systems have evolved more as financing systems than for regulating traffic. The city of Trondheim started with a toll station that charged all traffic that went through town. The motorists did not have to pay the charge if they used the road around the town, with no need to enter central areas. A significant share of the traffic was motivated to take this road around central areas. It was then decided to charge this traffic too for financial reasons, and thereby the incentives to move around the city centre became lower.

We have also gained experience from toll roads leading into the larger cities in Norway with toll levels significantly higher than in the toll rings. In Trondheim, one main road has a toll station with a charge of ECU 2.5 extra to enter the town. This main road has a parallel road leading downtown which prolongs travel time by 6-7 minutes. The experience here is that 60 per cent of the traffic will choose the longer route. This has caused the toll company large financial problems (implicit value of time through revealed preference analyses give figures somewhat higher than "state of the art" (Tretvik, 1992)). They will now have to close this alternative road for those other than locals. This is a very difficult political problem to solve. In the meantime, the debt grows very rapidly. This is a kind of race between growing debts and the barriers in the political decision process.

We also have experience from roads leading into towns where tolls have been very high (ECU 6-7 per passage). Several projects have ended up with great financial problems because the infrastructure is private and based on revenue from tolls. When this situation occurs it is very difficult to find a proper solution. The experience shows that it is not possible to increase prices to give a sufficient increase in income. Price rise in a system with initially high prices causes a relatively large traffic decrease (and repetitive price rises enlarge the traffic rejection because the price elasticity rises) (Hervik and Braathen, 1992). Public support to private infrastructure companies in crisis will be unacceptable because of incentive problems to private risk taking in general. The learning process has been not to base income on uncertain prognoses and high price level, but to look upon these projects just like other uncertain investments and take market uncertainty into the decision process. When pricing in toll stations passes a certain level, the market reactions seem to be more significant than what we see in low priced toll stations.

The cross-price elasticities towards public transport seem to be much higher when we come to these high level toll roads. In Norway, this leads to charging public transport as well because the shift from car use can lead to financial problems. Today, public transport is not charged in any of the toll rings, but usually pays on most high priced toll roads.

Up to now we have not discussed parking charges as a part of a charging system for the use of infrastructure. The parking areas will be defined as a part of the infrastructure itself, but it is also possible to develop a charging system for parking where you also pay a certain fee for using the roads leading to parking areas. This can be done by having much higher fees for parking in peak hours rather than in off-peak hours. With high charges it could be possible to charge also for the use of the road system. Many cities make use of parking charges as a measure to regulate traffic. The experience is that, even though it is more commonly used than tolls today to regulate traffic, it does not prove to be very efficient in most cases. The reason is that it is still very difficult to integrate all private parking into the charging system. There also seems to be a tradition that parking charges are payed by the employer and not by the traveller himself. This charging system does not influence the traffic going through the central areas with no need for parking. It is not a system where you pay for the infrastructure costs according to marginal cost because you will have the same parking charge whether you travel a road with heavy congestion or not. Charging the parking infrastructure with parking fees including charges for congested road use is developing into an important measure in many urban areas. High parking charges and limited space for parking will not be the most efficient charging system for the use of urban infrastructure. In a "second best" world this can be the only possible alternative in some places to supplementing fuel tax with a "quasi" toll ring system.

Much experience has been gained from the licence system in Singapore. The system has not yet been introduced any other place. A similar system might now be introduced in Cambridge where, in addition to paying a licence to enter a certain region, you also pay for the period you stay in that region. The licence system can look very similar to a toll ring system where you also pay to enter a region. The main difference might be the paying mechanism. Today, it is easy to see that some kind of toll rings with electronic charging systems will have the technology with the best possibility to regulate traffic according to the main long term objectives.

The annual registration fee is often not included as a traffic regulating charging system. It is most common to treat this as a part of the general taxation. Another possibility is to look at the annual fee as a part of the total charging system, as the fixed charge you have to pay to have access to the infrastructure. If the annual fee is differentiated between different regions (higher in urban areas with very high infrastructure costs and higher quality public transport systems than in rural areas), this can influence the growth in car density. Once the annual fee has been paid, it gives no incentive to car use. However, the annual fee can be developed into a two-tariff system with one annual fee and a payment for each time you enter a certain area during peak hours. As discussed earlier, this "licence" system can today be more efficiently developed by an electronically based toll road system.

4. ROAD PRICING

Road pricing is the charging system where each link is charged according to short-run marginal costs where differences in short-run marginal capacity costs will vary significantly between links and time. The charging system will be highly differentiated. The system costs will be high because of the need to install an electronic system in a very complex road system. The perfect road pricing system will also give a charging system where there will be no room for fuel tax (except as general taxation). Even if the electronic system is available, it will be an expensive charging system if we strive for the perfect road pricing system. The main principles from road pricing can, however, still be guidelines for the second best system: fuel tax combined with toll roads and toll rings. The toll system should be developed towards road pricing principles, especially by differentiating the charges according to short-run marginal capacity costs, with significantly higher prices on certain links during peak hours.

Road pricing should still be the optimal principle for the future charging system and the second best charging system should develop towards this system in the long run.

Only a road pricing system can prevent incentives to overinvestment or investments in bad projects. When the market pays the right price according to the principles of road pricing we have a guarantee that cost-benefit analyses will give the correct decision criteria.

Figure 3 illustrates a transport system where we have the right toll equal to AB. If all alternative routes are also priced equal to short-term marginal cost then we only need to look at this partial road system when evaluating costs and benefits for new investments. With no road pricing system it will be necessary

25

to look at changes in the total transport system to calculate the total relevant costs and benefits. This total analysis will in most cases be very complex and uncertain as a decision criterion (Mohring, 1976). In Figure 3 we have assumed that the demand is completely elastic beyond point A (Newbery, 1991). If we now choose to invest in new infrastructure we will have a new equilibrium in point C with optimal tolls CD. Total revenue from tolls is ACDB and this will also be equal to the extra benefit from all the users of this new infrastructure. If the infrastructure has constant benefit according to scale, and the new infrastructure is self-financed, then the total benefit will equal total costs and equal the total revenue from the extra traffic generated by the new infrastructure. The main idea is that with optimal road pricing it is much easier to use ordinary investment criteria, and toll revenue will cover investment costs in optimum. This is not the case when there is no road pricing, and much more complicated analytical criteria are the required.

With no charging systems in urban areas we very easily run into the problem described as early as in 1967 (Vichery, 1967):

"There are probably few areas in modern economic society where conditions are as far from ideal as in the congested traffic and transportation facilities of our great modern metropolitan conurbations. This is equally true in the short-run, in terms of making the best use of the facilities we have, and in the longer run, in terms of the appropriateness of the facilities for current and projected traffic needs. This relative inefficiency can be attributed in large measure to the fact that the individual user, faced with alternative ways of achieving his objectives, does not, under existing conditions, receive any obvious indication of the costs which his choice will impose on others, whether by impairment of the quality of service or by the cost of expanding the facilities to the point where this impairment is prevented.

To begin with it is perhaps worth observing that sometimes a facility becomes worthless precisely because it is free. For example, where a high-speed or short-cut facility of limited capacity has as an alternative a more circuitous or slower route with ample capacity, free operation may mean that a queue builds up during heavy demand periods at the access to the faster facility until the time required for queuing and transit is equal to the transit time by the circuitous route; under these circumstances no-one is able to make the trip any faster than if the faster route did not exist. Enlargement of the faster route may be a complete waste of money unless the route is enlarged sufficiently to take care of all traffic that might offer."

26

Wardrop's third principle (Wardrop, 1952) can be formulated as (Holden, 1989):

"Traffic will tend to settle down into an equilibrium situation in which no driver can reduce his journey time by choosing a new route."

Figure 4 illustrates this problem. The number of cars travelling AB will equal Q1 because the queues will give exactly the travelling time equal to travelling by train. Travelling time by train is fixed. Developing new infrastructure is illustrated by the new equilibrium Q2 moving from E1 to E2. Travelling time will still be the same as that defined by the travelling time by train. However, more people will travel by car illustrated by the increase Q2-Q1. The next problem might be that the traffic decrease from train might imply that one must reduce the service level, e.g. by a lower frequency of trains in peak hours. This could lead to increased travelling time by train. The new equilibrium point could now be E3 increasing car traffic to Q3 with the consequence that travelling time has increased to the higher level defined by travelling time by rail.

We shall now return to a road pricing system for Oslo to illustrate the allocation loss from having no optimal road pricing system during peak hours. We can segment the commuter market in Oslo and construct a simple model simulating demand and supply functions in different market segments (Larsen, 1990). We will present the model as a simple aggregated version illustrated in Figure 5 (Hervik and Brunstad, 1992). As an average, we have in equilibrium 25 000 cars per hour travelling into Oslo. The average generalised cost is NKr 65. Demand E1 illustrates the level when we have no queues and E2 the demand in peak hours. The optimal toll is calculated to be 25 NKr. The allocation loss by not introducing road pricing is illustrated by the cross-hatched area in the figure and represents NKr 140 million a year. The marginal shadow price (CD) or the allocation loss on the marginal car is stipulated as being NKr 50.

This model has many uncertainties and Table 4 shows how the allocation loss varies with the assumption of price elasticities and the optimal toll. If, for instance, the environmental external costs are stipulated to be some NKr 5 higher (optimum toll is then NKr 30) and the price elasticity is - 0.9 (in generalised costs) and not - 0.7 as a main assumption, then the allocation loss increases with more than a factor of 4 to NKr 607. The price elasticity will among other factors depend on the standard of public transportation. Variations in value of time and the traffic level travelling into Oslo in peak hours is not that sensitive in this calculation. The total allocation loss depends most of all on how we value environmental costs (and accident costs) in urban areas and the price elasticity including the standard of public transportation. A high standard will cause car users to swap to public transport with an increase in tolls, and the allocation loss will then be high if prices in public transport are not increased to cover marginal costs. Most calculations of allocation costs will estimate a figure of what the total congestion costs will be. This figure will be much higher than the allocation loss because of the lack of road pricing. In equilibrium, there will still be queues in urban areas as shown in Figure 5, and the correct allocation loss is the cross-hatched area in the figure and not total congestion costs.

The simple model we have used in our illustrations throughout this paper is theoretically not strictly correct. This is shown by Small (1992) and Arnott, Palma and Lindsey (1993) in a very recent paper in *The American Economic Review*. The new "structural" models focus on the user's behavioural decisions and trade-off between the cost of using the infrastructure at an inconvenient time against the congestion cost when it is crowded. The "structural" models also focus on congestion technology and dynamic perspective and give more complex analytical charts than the simple one we have used.

These recent works conclude that the allocation loss from lack of road pricing in urban areas may have been substantially underestimated by traditional methods. However, the simple figures we have used illustrate the main aspects of the topic of charging systems, and the fundamental economic principles in this economic analysis are not influenced too much by the new models. Empirical studies of road pricing will, in the future, have to use this new analytical tool.

In Jones and Hervik (1992) where the topic was trends and barriers for road pricing, the conclusion was that some kind of road pricing will offer the best solution for restraining car traffic in many European cities. Despite recent political setbacks in some European countries (Netherlands and Sweden), trends in traffic growth and environmental issues are likely to increase the pressure for this type of measure. The most important crucial issues to be resolved are summarised in the following points:

"1. The need to address the issues of privacy, equity and allocation in a politically acceptable way, and to ensure effective enforcement and technological compatibility across Europe.

2. The long-term question concerning the effectiveness and impacts of a road pricing scheme: Will it be politically feasible to maintain the real value of the charge, and if necessary raise it in real terms in line with income growth? And, what will be the long-term land use implications?

3. The need to view road pricing as part of a comprehensive package of measures rather than a solution in its own right. A number of factors need to be considered here:

   i) The provision or facilitating of adequate alternatives to travelling by private car (both improved bus/rail systems and a safe cycle/pedestrian environment).
   ii) The introduction of flexible work hours and other institutional changes that would enable people to respond to the price mechanism by rescheduling their travel.
   iii) The alleviation of the secondary traffic effects that the simpler cordon-based road pricing schemes would generate, both inside and outside the restricted area. Within the area traffic speed may rise, leading to concerns about increased accidents, and outside the area there will be peripheral parking and network congestion problems to be resolved.

As European cities enter the 1990s, with the expectation of worse traffic conditions to come, the question is how rather than where these issues will be resolved. The present indications are that traffic restraint will become an active ingredient of urban transport policy in many European cities, and that under certain conditions some form of road pricing will offer the best solution. Despite recent political setbacks in some European countries, the growing concern with global warming issues is likely to increase the pressure for this type of measure."

5. CHARGING SYSTEMS FOR PUBLIC TRANSPORT URBAN INFRASTRUCTURES

Urban railways operate in most countries as public sector monopolies. They are managed as integrated businesses combining both infrastructure and services. In most countries this system is heavily subsidised, and because of this institutional integration there is no such charging system for urban infrastructure like marginal cost pricing. To introduce a charging system for use of infrastructure, one crucial step is to separate tracks and associated signalling from rolling stock and transport services.

As for marginal cost pricing for roads, it is difficult to estimate precisely the cost caused by different types of rolling stock using the infrastructure. This will include maintenance costs and accident and environmental costs. The example from Sweden shows that it is possible to give rough estimates for these costs. The charging system is separated into fixed and variable charges. The variable charges vary between different locomotives and between different links. The fixed charges are equivalent to road vehicle taxes. One main motivation for this institutional change is to ensure there is one operator with pure commercial interests and one responsible for the infrastructure where all investment will be based on cost/benefit analyses.

The charging system should reflect the competition between rail and road. As for roads, it is only under "correct" prices that costs and benefits of new investment in tracks can be calculated in a straightforward manner. The charging system for the infrastructure will also be a financial source for these investments. Contrary to road charges, charging rail will not be sufficient to cover all costs.

The same system introduced in Sweden in 1990 has now been introduced in Norway. The European Commission has also made proposals to disentangle service and infrastructure to introduce a measure to equalise competition between road and rail.

Tolls, or a system similar to road pricing, is a necessary precondition for a rational charging system for rail infrastructure in urban areas. If vehicles are not charged according to their marginal costs, it will not be rational to charge the rail system according to marginal costs either. The calculation problems in urban areas with great congestions in the second best world are very complex for pinpointing the most efficient economic investment. Without marginal cost pricing this will be a total system analysis. The more theoretical and empirical analyses concerning charging systems for rail infrastructure should be that the system should give great differentiations between time and areas according to variations in demand. This will be a conclusion independent of price level and implicit the subsidy level (Jan Owen Jansson, *et al.*, 1990).

6. CONCLUSION

Charging systems for the use of urban infrastructure are well developed as a theoretical topic but the political barriers for implementing "the optimal" system appear to be overwhelming. The experience from Norway focuses on toll rings as a measure for financing new urban infrastructure. The decision process shows that it is important to have a package when introducing tolls consisting of a fair discount system. Local authorities must have incentives to introduce the charging system. Road pricing will give the efficiency criteria that all "second best" systems should aim at. The more "practical" charging systems will be some kind of combination between petrol tax and toll rings/roads in most countries in the near future. The latter part of this charging system in urban areas should not only be a source for financing new infrastructure, but developed to regulate traffic. This means differentiating the charge for different periods and between different roads according to demand variations. The experiences in Norway with toll rings around all major cities are very positive and the equipment for electronic payment functions very well.

Even when this charging system is introduced in toll rings, much remains to be done to develop the charging system for urban infrastructure to regulate traffic. The alternative charging systems with parking fees and differentiated petrol tax do not have the same possibilities and flexibility as an efficient charging system for urban infrastructure.

TABLES

Table 1. **Classification of road user charging systems**

Acquisition Fees (on vehicles)	Ownership Fees (on vehicles; usually annual)	Indirect Use Fees	Direct Use Fees
Sales tax	Registration fee	Fuel tax	Bridge tolls
Value-added tax (VAT)	Personal property tax	Supplementary area licence	Roadway tolls
Transfer tax	Driving licence fee	Cordon tolls	Automatically metered tolls (road pricing) - on-vehicle - off-vehicle
			Weight-distance fees on heavy vehicles

Table 2. **Indirect road user charges (fuel and vehicle taxes) in selected European countries (ECU million, 1986)**

Country	Revenue from:				Expenditure on roads	Revenue as % of expenditure
	Fuel tax	Vehicle taxes	Tolls	Total		
Belgium	1 014	320	-	1 334	1 777	75
Denmark	455	280	-	735	751	98
Germany	7 936	2 623	-	10 559	11 029	96
Greece	473	97	1	571	334	171
France	6 342	1 054	1 135	8 531	6 413	133
Ireland	304	28	-	332	213	156
Italy	5 155	420	712	6 287	3 464	181
Luxembourg	57	9	-	66	101	66
Netherlands	1 151	809	-	1 960	2 310	85
Portugal	244	18	-	262	na	na
UK	5 504	2 212	-	7 716	4 286	180
EC Total (exc. Spain)	**28 635**	**7 870**	**1 848**	**38 353**	**30 678** (exc. Spain & Portugal)	**124** (exc. Spain & Portugal)

Source: European Commission: "Elimination of Distortions of Competition of a Fiscal Nature in the Transport of Goods by Road", 1986.

Table 3. Fuel prices and fuel taxes in selected countries in the third quarter 1991 (NKr/litre)

Country	Leaded fuel		Diesel	
	Price	Tax [2]	Price	Tax
Belgium	5.96	3.95	3.49	1.63
Denmark	6.18	4.17	3.12	1.12
Finland	7.11	4.35	4.93	2.59
France	6.24	4.63	3.46	1.95
Italy	8.03	6.05	4.90	3.27
Netherlands	7.10	5.08	3.38	1.68
Norway	7.13	4.47	2.78	0.69
Portugal	6.66	4.79	4.22	2.48
Spain	5.57	3.63	3.83	2.02
UK	5.80	3.85	4.35	2.53
Sweden	7.39	4.98	4.24	1.36
Switzerland	4.98	2.95	4.76	2.86
Germany	6.25	4.37	3.75	2.13
USA [1]	2.37	0.71	2.00	0.70
Austria	5.55	3.18	3.89	1.83
OECD, Europe	6.27	-	3.94	-
OECD, Total	3.23	-	3.07	-

(1)   Price and tax for unleaded fuel.
(2)   Including VAT.

Source: IEA: Energy prices and taxes, third quarter 1991.

Table 4. Sensitivity analyses of changes in road charges and price elasticities (NKr)

Price elasticities e_{11}	Optimal road charges B:		
	20	25	30
-0.5	46	90	169
-0.7	65	138	315
-0.9	83	198	607

FIGURES

Figure 1. **Marginal and average costs of city street trips**

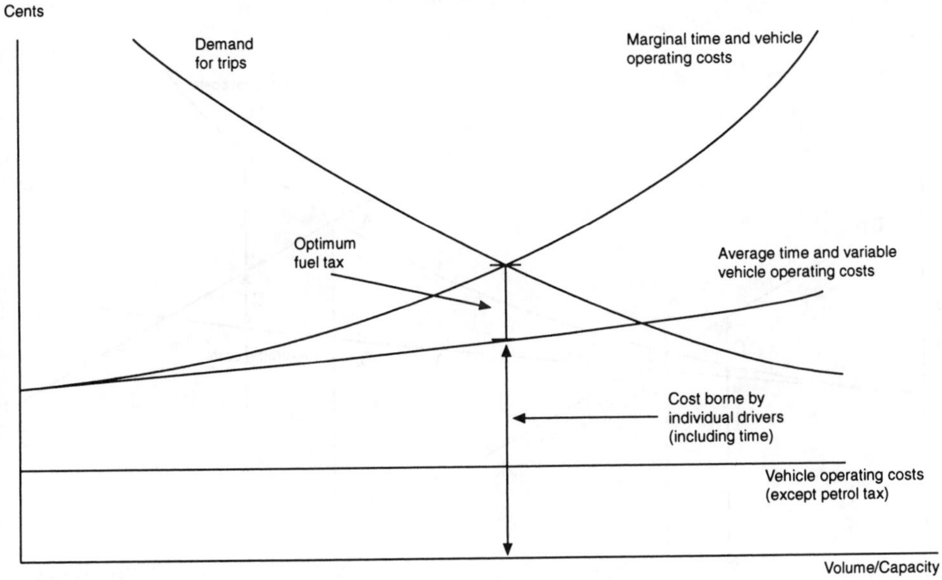

Cents

Demand
for trips

Marginal time and vehicle
operating costs

Optimum
fuel tax

Average time and variable
vehicle operating costs

Cost borne by
individual drivers
(including time)

Vehicle operating costs
(except petrol tax)

Volume/Capacity

41

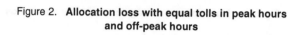

Figure 2. **Allocation loss with equal tolls in peak hours and off-peak hours**

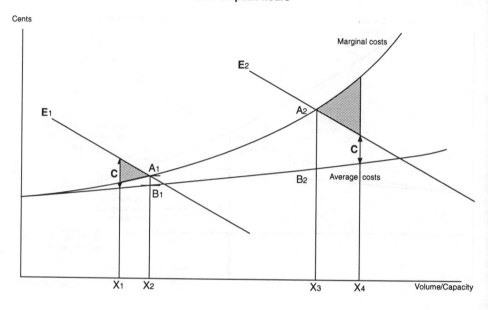

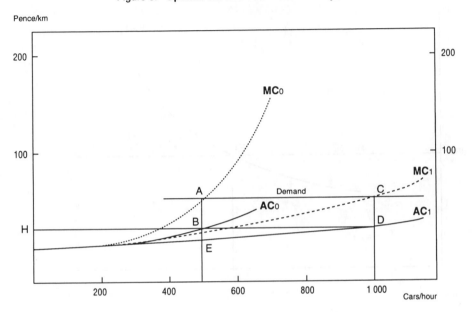

Figure 3. **Optimal toll and cost-benefit analysis**

43

Figure 4. **Equilibrium travelling time and shift of equilibrium**

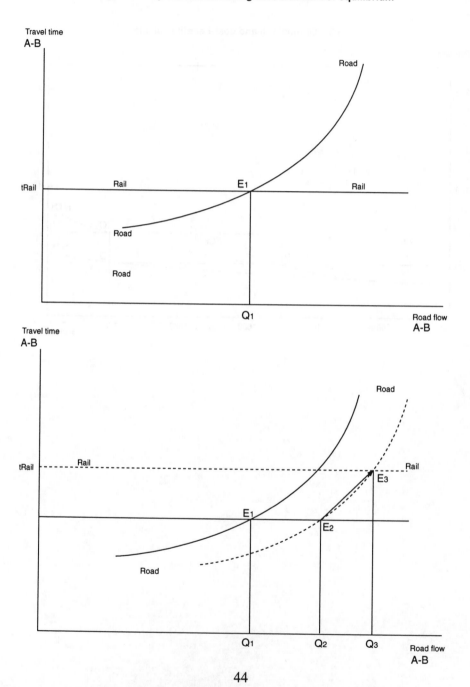

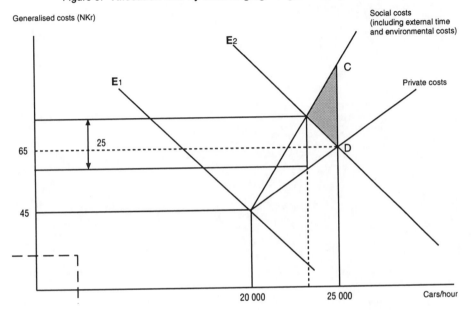

Figure 5. **Allocation loss by not charging marginal cost prices in Oslo**

Generalised costs (NKr)

Social costs
(including external time
and environmental costs)

E₂

C

E₁

Private costs

25

65

45

20 000   25 000   Cars/hour

D

45

ANNEX

A BRIEF PRESENTATION OF THE TRONDHEIM TOLL RING

This chapter gives a brief presentation of the charging system in the Trondheim toll ring. The toll ring operates the most complex electronic charging system implemented in Norway (and throughout Europe) and this system (developed and manufactured in Norway) can be considered technically as "State of the Art". The system consists of several electronic unmanned stations (except for two major stations which also cover non-local traffic). Electronic charging implies that no stopping is required. Cars are identified and charged by identifying a chip inside the windscreen when passing through. A video system is established to detect and prevent non-paying driving. The chip itself is free, and discount is achieved from the first trip on. This has been done as a measure to minimise manual payment, which requires stopping and increases charging costs. Yet manual payment is possible, even in stations without crew -- one has to push a button, get a bill and pay in a post office. The electronic system is unable to charge passengers.

The main purpose for the toll ring in Trondheim is fiscal. There was a certain political resistance from local authorities, and a great effort was made to create a charging system which was politically feasible.

The charging system in Trondheim:

--   The charging period ("opening time") is between 6.00 a.m. -- 5.00 p.m. The period 5.00 p.m. -- 6.00 a.m. and during weekends is free. Travellers can choose between manual and electronic payment.
--   There were about 21 million vehicles passing through the toll ring in 1992 during "opening time". This is about 50 per cent of the total volume.
--   The manual charge is ECU 1.25 for cars. No discounts. No passenger fees. Trucks pay twice this amount.
--   The electronic system charges each trip. Users of this system ("chip-holders") can either use prepayment (varies between ECU 62.50

and ECU 625) or allow direct transfer from the traveller's bank account (AUTOGIRO).

-- Within *peak hours* the electronic charge is ECU 1.0 (between 6.00 -- 10.00 a.m. and between 2.00 -- 5.00 p.m.). Trucks pay twice this amount.

-- In *off-peak hours* the discounts in the electronic system vary between 30 per cent and 50 per cent (the charge varies between ECU 0.50 and ECU 0.70) The discount depends on the size of the lump-sum prepayment (varies between ECU 62.50 (discount 30 per cent) and ECU 625 (discount 50 per cent). AUTOGIRO gives a discount of 30 per cent.

-- In the charging periods there is an upper limit of 1 payment/hour and 75 payments/ month for users of the electronic system. If these limits are exceeded, no charges are made for extra trips. The maximum payments during a month (commuter travelling in peak hours) therefore amount to ECU 75 for cars.

Implications of the system:

-- There is a very modest element of peak-load pricing present (no discount in peak hours). This fee is not imposed on an empirical base of the necessary level of peak pricing.

-- There are some queuing-up because of stopping just before 5.00 pm (just before passing is free of charge), but this has not led to severe congestion problems around the stations. From the same reason there is a noticeable traffic peak just after 5.00 pm.

-- Very few users reach the limit of 75 payments/month.

-- 80 per cent of the users prefer the electronic charging system. 70 per cent of these users prefer AUTOGIRO instead of lump-sum prepayment, even if lump-sum payment of ECU 312 (covers about 4 months commuting in peak hours) and higher implies a larger discount.

The revenues from the toll ring are about ECU 8.75 million per annum, which is sufficient to cover the mortgage on completed projects. The infrastructure plan for the Trondheim area contains several projects not yet completed. Following this plan requires annual revenues of about ECU 12.5, which is a rise of approximately 45 per cent according to the present level of income. The traffic volume is no doubt sufficient to provide such level of income. There is now a strategic discussion (in its early stage) on how to achieve this income level.

Actual measures might be:

-- Reduce the limit of one payment per hour to one payment per 30 min.;
-- 24 hours charging period (or at least some prolongation);
-- General price rise.

BIBLIOGRAPHY

Arnott, Richard, de Palma, Andre and Lindsey, Robin: "A Structural Model of Peak-Period Congestion: A Traffic Bottleneck with Elastic Demand." *The American Economic Review*, March 1993.

Berechman, Joseph: "Transportation Policy in Europe" *Transportation Research*, Vol. 26A, No. 2, March 1992.

Bovy, P.H.L.: "Infrastructure Planning as a Part of The Second Dutch Transport Structure Plan" Ministry of Transport and Public Works, Rijkswaterstaat, Traffic and Transport Research Division, The Netherlands, 1991.

Bræin, L., Hervik, A., Warnes, A.B.: "Markedsanalyse for kollektivtransport ved store endringer i relative priser. Forprosjekt" *Arbeidsrapport* M 9116, Møreforsking Molde, Norway, 1991.

European Round Table of Industrialists: "Missing Network. A European Challenge".

Goodwin, P.B. and Jones, P.M.: Road Pricing: "The Political and Strategic Possibilities" Round Table 80: Systems of road infrastructure cost coverage, ECMT, February 1989.

Hervik, Arild: "Et samfunnsøkonomisk perspektiv på kollektivtransporten", NORAS, *Nasjonalt FoU-program for kollektivtransport* (Report No. 7) Oslo, Norway, 1992.

Hervik, Arild: "Nytte-kostnadsanalyse i vegsektoren" Paper til 14. *Forskermøte for økonomer*. Handelshøyskolen BI, Oslo, Norway, January 1992.

Hervik, Arild, Brunstad, Rolf J.: "Sentraliseringens pris i trafikkmarkedet. SNF-prosjekt 235: Samfunnsøkonomiske konsekvenser av sentralisering", *Arbeidsnotat* nr. 18/1992, Bergen, Norway, 1992.

Hervik, A. and Braathen, S.: "Ökonomiske analyser av nye bru/tunnelprosjekter" Working paper M9003, Møreforsking Molde, Norway, 1990.

Holden, David J.: "Wardrop's Third Principle. Urban Traffic. Congestion and Traffic Policy". *Journal of Transport Economics and Policy*, September 1992.

Jansson, J.O. and Cardebring, P.: "Developments in Transport Policy. Swedish railway Policy 1979-88", *Journal of Transport Economics and Policy*, September 1989.

Jansson, J.O., Sonesson, T. and Andersson, P: "Hur mycket bör det kosta att åka tåg?", Ekonomisk Debatt 1/90, Sweden, 1990.

Jansson, K. and Wallin, B.: "Developments in Transport Policy. Deregulation of Public Transport in Sweden". *Journal of Transport Economics and Policy*, January 1991.

Jørgensen, L., Philaja, M., Bjørgan T., Westlie, N., Tegner, G.: "Avgiftsordninger i byer" *Nordisk Vegteknisk forbund*, Ad-hoc utvalg: Transport i større byer, Rapport nr. 16/1992 Oslo, Norway, 1992.

Johnston, R. A. and DeLuchi, M. A.: "Evaluation Method for Rail Transit Projects", *Transportation Research-A*, Vol. 23A No. 4, pp. 317-325, 1989.

Kågeson, Per: "Internalising Social Costs of Transport. A Preliminary study" *The European Federation for Transport and Environment*, SNF Stockholm, 1992.

Larsen, Odd I.: "Bompengeringen i Bergen -- erfaringer og virkninger på trafikken", Transportøkonomisk institutt, Oslo ISBN 82-7133-566-9, 1987.

Larsen, Odd I.: "Road Investment with Road Pricing -- Investment Criteria and the Revenue/Cost Issue." Institute of Transport Economics, Oslo, Norway, 1991.

Larsen, Odd I., Mathieu P. and Ramjerdi F.: "Is 'Perfect' Road Pricing Cost Efficient?", Institute of Transport Economics, Oslo, Norway, 1991.

Mohring, H. (1976): "Transportation Economics", London, Macmillan, 1981.

Newbery, David M.: "Road Users Charges in Britain", *The Economic Journal 98* (Conference 1988), 1988.

53

Newbery, David M.: "Pricing and Congestion: Economic Principles Relevant to Pricing Roads", *Oxford Review of Economic Policy*, Vol. 6, No. 2, 1991.

OECD: "Co-ordinated Urban Transport Pricing" OECD, Paris, 1985.

Rekening Rijden Project-team: "Road pricing in The Netherlands", Ministry of Transport and Public Works, The Netherlands.

Small, Kenneth A.: "Urban Transport Economics", Harwood Academic Publishers, 1992.

Solheim, Trygve: "Bompengeringen i Oslo: effekter på trafikk og folks reisevaner", Transportøkonomisk institutt, TØI-rapport nr. 126/92, Oslo, Norway, 1992.

St.meld. nr.34 (1992-93) "Norsk veg- og vegtrafikkplan 1994-97", Samferdselsdepartementet, Oslo, Norway, 1993.

Tretvik, Terje: "Modelling Car Driver Responses to Route Tolls" SINTEF Transport Engineering Trondheim, Norway, 1991.

NETHERLANDS

H. POL
Ministry of Transport and Public Works
The Hague
Netherlands

This contribution has been written in a personal capacity. The author is solely responsible for the views presented in this paper, which do not (necessarily) reflect the views or policies of the Dutch Ministry of Transport and Public Works.

SUMMARY

Delft, May 1993

INTRODUCTION

This contribution to the subject "Charging systems for the use of urban infrastructure" focuses on charging systems for the use of urban infrastructure by cars. It does not pay attention to charging systems in public transport, for use of telecom infrastructure, for the use of infrastructure by foot, bicycle and so on. The usage by cars can be twofold: driving and parking. By definition, parked cars stand still and this allows for simple and nowadays well-known charging mechanisms. For this reason, the focus of this contribution will be on systems for charging moving motor vehicles for the use of urban infrastructure.

It is important to note that charging (for the use of urban infrastructure) is not done for the sake of charging itself. Charging is only done to reach certain (policy) goals. Starting from these goals in many cases there are different potential measures to reach the goal. Whether or not charging is the optimal measure for reaching the goal is beyond the scope of this contribution. Weighing all possible measures may lead to the conclusion that charging is not suitable; that all in all another measure is more fit for the purpose. The starting point for this contribution is that charging can play a role to reach certain goals. This contribution explores the characteristics of such charging.

The possible objectives of charging will be explored in Chapter 1. Charging systems will be treated in Chapters 2 and 3. In Chapter 2 the principles and in Chapter 3 the technical aspects of charging systems will be analysed. Chapter 4 brings together the objectives and the charging systems and identifies the preferred system(s) as function of the desired objectives. Chapter 4 may be regarded as the core chapter of the contribution. Chapter 5 deals with specific requirements for urban charging systems, while Chapter 6 gives an overview of the European standardization of automatic debiting systems (ADS). The final chapter, Chapter 7, contains the conclusions.

1. OBJECTIVE OF CHARGING

Charging systems for the use of urban infrastructure are being implemented to achieve a certain goal or set of goals. Later on it will be made clear that there is a relation between the objective of charging and the appropriate charging system(s). Therefore in this first chapter an analysis will be made of the possible objectives of charging.

1.1. The transport market

Pricing and charging can play a role in organising the transport market. In Figure 1 the three angles that determine the "Transport Triangle" are given. In some sense the Transport Triangle is a reflection of the transport market forces.

"User demand" stands for the demand to make trips to be able to fulfil the need to take part in a certain activity that is spatially separated from the actual origin of the user.

"Suppliers" are suppliers of road space (for driving and parking) as well as suppliers of public transport, telecom facilities, etc.

In a perfect market, supply and demand meet unrestricted. Privately owned, non-subsidised bus systems are an example of (a part of) such a situation.

Pricing plays a substantial role in organising the "perfect market".

In general, passenger traffic is not a perfect market. There are "limiting conditions" for demand and supply to meet. One of the main limiting conditions is the external effects of transport, which are not internalised in the price of the supplier's product. External effects of the car system are amongst others:

-- Noise;
-- Smells;
-- Use of space in urban areas;
-- Splitting up of ground by roads (roads becoming social barriers and dividing the living space both for man and animal);
-- Emissions of harmful particles (NOx, CxHy, COx, dust);
-- Using non-replaceable energy sources.

Another element of the imperfection of the market is the fact that an individual user influences the performance of the system for (all) other users, without being confronted with the costs for the other users (marginal societal costs). This imperfection is most apparent as usage is near system capacity. A next user causes the whole system to slow down. This leads to extra costs for all present users, but the "last" user is not confronted with these costs. The "last" user is only confronted with the actual (costs of) systems performance at this moment and decides whether or not to enter the system based on these individual mean costs. When this user decides then to enter the system, as a consequence the costs for all present users rise. The decision process of an individual car user to enter the system is not optimal from a systems point of view.

Charging can be used to reach a market situation that takes into account the limiting conditions that exist for car usage.

1.1.1. Some examples

To arrange the processes in the Transport Triangle, charging/pricing is one possible tool. By way of illustration, two examples of the role of charging/pricing will be given here.

Payment to supplier

The first application of charging (pricing) is to pay for the services of a supplier. The supplier may, for instance, be a toll road company, building and maintaining road space and charging users for the usage of the road. Other examples are: fares for ferries and car park tariffs. The objective of charging here is to make good the costs of the supplier. At a certain price customers are willing to use the service. That is where demand and supply meet.

Regulating

In circumstances where the equilibrium between demand and supply does not conform to any "externally" desired situation, the third angle of the Transport Triangle is activated. This will be illustrated by urban parking.

The availability of parking space is an essential condition for the functioning of cities. If parking space is not regulated, typically most of it will be occupied by residents' and commuters' cars. There will hardly be any parking space left for shopping and business traffic (staff meetings, representatives, distribution of goods, etc.). Such a situation encourages firms to leave cities; the city deteriorates. This is where parking policy comes into life.

61

Some parking space has to be "reserved" for special purposes, e.g. for business traffic. Here we can use charging. By supplying some parking space at a very high tariff a situation can be realised where in general parking space will always be available for business travellers. Due to the high tariff, long parking (residents, commuters) is made unattractive and "marginal travel" will not be prepared to pay the high tariff for using these parking places. By levying high parking tariffs, the accessibility of firms -- and the functioning of the city -- can be guaranteed. [In some parts of The Hague in recent years parking tariffs up to ƒ 8 per hour (= 3.7 ECU/hour) have been introduced. This has led to the situation that business travellers always find some empty parking places. Searching for parking space and walking long distances from the parking space to the firm's address -- costing time, money and frustration -- are no longer necessary.]

The objective of charging in the parking example is to realise a desired (parking) policy. Tariffs here are not so much a function of the real costs, but are related to the policy goals; in practice they exceed the real costs.

1.2. Transport policy goals in urban areas

Typically, in urban areas there is an accumulation of activities. Employment, shopping, leisure and housing are packed together, leading to a high density of activities per m^2. All these activities attract the public, which leads to massive traffic flows.

Typically, the traffic problems in cities are:

-- Traffic imposes a high environmental burden on the urban area;
-- Given the natural scarcity of space in urban areas, transport networks are congested;
-- Shortage of money to invest in (new) transport facilities.

In most urban areas, the transport policy goals towards the moving motor vehicles are therefore:

-- To reduce the environmental burden of traffic ("limiting conditions");
-- To improve accessibility ("meeting demand");
-- To reduce subsidies to the transport system ("let the market work").

1.3. Policy measures: the role of charging

To reach the policy goals set measures have to be taken. One of these measures can be charging. In this section an analysis is given of why charging is needed and where charging can be an attractive policy instrument.

1.3.1. Reduction of environmental burden

Reduction of the environmental burden was found to be one of the policy goals in urban areas. To reduce the environmental burden of (the car) traffic, the measures most popular with the general public are those that supply alternatives to overcome these problems. Traditionally, public transport is seen as such an alternative, but other measures exist as well. For instance Dutch transport policy [1] gives major attention to initiatives for tele-activities. Tele-working, for instance, means working at home or near home using telecommunication connected to the office. Tele-working two days a week may avoid four commuter trips; less trips lead to a smaller environmental burden. Other alternatives are facilities for car pooling, bicycling, etc.

Although popular with the public, experience in the Netherlands (and elsewhere in the western world) shows that the introduction/presence of alternatives does not attract many car users. They prefer using their own motor vehicle, even given the bad performance of the car system and the availability of good alternatives. It seems that the alternatives to a great extent attract new passengers, therefore generating extra mobility. *The effectiveness of supplying alternatives for the car, as far as reduction of car usage is concerned, is very limited*[1].

A second element in Dutch transport policy is therefore not only to supply alternatives, but to stimulate use of them in an active way. This means subsidising/facilitating alternatives, giving tax reductions in case of using alternatives, etc. Once again only a small number of car users is persuaded to use the alternatives. Again the effectiveness is very limited. *Only supplying alternatives and stimulating usage is not enough to reduce the **environmental burden** of traffic.*

This leads to the conclusion that, unavoidably, the car itself must be tackled in order to reach the desired policy goal. In general, measures to tackle the car itself are firmly turned down by (a part of) the public and the automobile lobby. This causes great reserve on the part of politicians in taking the adequate measures. However, the best policy here is to reach a situation whereby cars become much cleaner and much more fuel-efficient in use and that they are produced in such a way that over the lifetime of a car the environmental burden is negligible. The most appropriate way to reach such a situation is to introduce -- Europe-wide or even world-wide -- very tough standards for allowing cars onto the market (100 per cent recycling; 0 per cent harmful gases; usage under 1 litre per 50 kilometres). If these demands are met, the environmental burden (except possibly the noise problem) can be reduced to acceptable levels.

However, even if tomorrow tough standards for new cars are introduced, it will take much time to reach the desired environmental situation. In the meantime, charging can be used to reduce the magnitude of the environmental pollution and fuel consumption. By making the use of the car more expensive there will be a reduction in car usage. This reduction leads to a reduction of the environmental burden. Charging for environmental reasons calls for a general/overall charge on every kilometre driven. A higher fuel price can do the job here.

1.3.2. *Improving accessibility*

Still, even a clean car will use space, both for driving and being parked. In urban areas the space on, over and under ground level is limited. Therefore the capacity in urban areas for dispatching cars will always be limited[2].

Two problems can be foreseen therefore:

-- Congestion in peak hours;
-- Overall congestion.

To improve accessibility -- given that alternatives are already available and attractive to use, as described before -- three further types of measures are available.

-- Pricing;
-- Legal regulations (mandates, prohibitions);
-- Physical measures.

All measures should lead to a reduction of demand for road space to avoid congestion.

Pricing

When demand is high, the price for using the road should be set at a level such that the equilibrium between demand and supply is reached without congestion. Pricing has the advantage that no-one is forbidden to use the car. Pricing does not make use of the car impossible, but usage has its price. Second, the (determination of the) price of car usage is brought in line with the determination of prices for consumption of other goods in society.

Legal regulations

Legal regulations to prevent congestion may take the form of odd-even number plate systems, in use in several cities in the world. These systems do have drawbacks in the sense that they are necessarily coarse and oversimplified. Legal regulations can never deal in an efficient way with, for example, "human needs", "urgency of transports", etc. Next to this, legal regulations need to be enforced; in practice this means a large number of personnel is needed and costs are high.

Physical measures

Physical measures to make car usage (at certain times/places) impossible are attractive from an enforcement point of view. Strong barricades "guarantee" the enforcement. The setback is -- even more than with legal regulations -- the oversimplified character of the measure. Car usage is made impossible for everybody, independent of how necessary or desired the car usage in fact may be. Furthermore, implementing such a measure in an existing[3] city may cause unacceptable effects. In an existing situation there will always be firms, etc. which need to be accessible by car. If this is no longer possible, such activities will leave the area; the area becomes less attractive.

Pricing seems to be the most attractive of the three, when the policy goal is to improve accessibility.

1.3.3. Reducing subsidies

In many cases road building and maintenance, traffic police, etc. are financed by the common means of municipalities, regions and so on. These costs may be seen as subsidies to the car users[4]. A measure to reduce these subsidies may be to pass on (more of) the costs to the user. It is clear that the instrument of charging/pricing is very relevant here. Passing on costs can, for instance, be done by tolling. In urban areas tolling is so far almost only done for expensive pieces of road, such as bridges and tunnels.

The other side of reducing subsidies is to generate funds for new investments in the transport system, by charging future users/beneficiaries in advance. The

Oslo situation can be mentioned here [2]. In February 1990, a toll ring around the city was put into operation. All incoming motor vehicles pay a fixed amount (person/cars: NKr 11 = 1.3 ECU) per passage. The revenue is used to build fifty infrastructure projects that, without the toll scheme, would be built much later. All taxed passages will benefit in some way -- now or in the future -- from the completion of the fifty projects. A small percentage of the revenue goes to public transport.

1.4. Objectives of charging

In Chapter 1 the relation between policy goals and pricing was analysed. Pricing urban infrastructure is not done without reason. It has been shown that next to the traditional tolling, pricing can play a role in reaching other traffic policy goals.

To sum up, charging in urban areas can be used to:

-- Improve accessibility by reducing the level of car usage at peak periods;
-- Pass on the costs of infrastructure (tolls/parking fees);
-- Generate funds (income);

and as an intermediate solution for:

-- Reducing the environmental burden by reducing the overall level of car usage.

So, in conclusion, pricing can be seen as an important and unavoidable policy tool to achieve the policy goals set.

1.5. Revenue

Seeing that the instrument used when charging is money, a product of charging is the revenue. When the charge is meant to raise funds there is no problem in allocating the revenue. When, on the other hand, the policy goal is to reduce car usage, nothing is fixed as far as the allocation of the revenue is concerned. However, using this revenue for any other purpose than giving it back to the (ex-)car users can not be motivated properly and will cause severe societal restraint towards introduction of the measure. Furthermore, giving back the money can avoid a situation of cost compensation by employers (possibly reducing the effect of the measure) and can solve possible problems of an (income) distributional type. That is why the author believes that the only practical way to deal with the revenue is to give it back to the (ex-)car users.

2. CHARGING SYSTEM

2.1. Introduction

In Chapter 1 the objectives of charging were analysed. There is a strong relationship between the objective and the system of charging, given the effectiveness of different charging systems. This chapter will analyse the different systems of charging. In a later chapter, objectives, systems and technical systems will be matched to preferred combinations. Figure 2 gives an overview of possible charging systems.

2.2. Analyses of charging systems

Charging systems can be divided into:

-- Usage-related systems;
-- Non usage-related systems.

Non usage-related

In charging systems that are not related to usage a more general charge for "using" the infrastructure is levied. The charge can be levied from all inhabitants of the urban area; from the owners of firms, operators of stores and so on or from the potential users of the urban infrastructure. When all inhabitants are charged, the charge takes the form of a local (urban) tax. Such a charge should be levied from the (car-owning) inhabitants of the urban area under discussion. This may be seen as unfair because people not living in the urban area but using the infrastructure there are not charged. Charging employers, shopkeepers, etc. may take the form of the *Versement Transport* that is levied in Paris. The charge is related to the total of wages paid (2 per cent) and is used for the infrastructure system (including public transport). Another base for this type of charging can be found in the number of visitors per year and so on. Non usage-related charging levied from potential users takes the form of (annual) taxation for possessing a car, taxation on the purchase of a car (new, second-hand) and so on.

Non usage-related charging must be seen as primarily to raise money (from motorists); the effects on car usage are negligible.

Usage-related

In systems with usage-related charging, the charge is related to the actual usage of the car, although that relation may be quite rudimentary in some systems. The relation with usage gives the opportunity to tailor the charge to specific objectives other than generating funds. Usage-related charging can be divided into:

-- Charging based on the total trip;
-- Charging based on parts of the trip.

Total trip

Charging the total trip takes the form of charging every kilometre. The tariff may be flat per km or related to the areas in which the trip is made and so on (Figure 2, box 7). Charging could also be done taking into account the specific Origin and Destination and Route of the trip (box 8). OD trips made in peak hours and for which excellent alternatives are available might be priced higher than other trips.

Part of trip

In these systems the whole trip is not charged, only part(s) of it; for instance those parts that lead through urban areas, use expensive stretches of road and so on. Charging based on part(s) of the total trip can be divided into systems where:

-- Payment is area-based; and where
-- Payment is based on the specific road sections used.

Area based

In these systems charging is related to the usage of infrastructure in a certain area. Area-based systems may take the form of a fixed payment for using roads in a certain area. For instance, driving in a section of the city centre costs a fixed amount per day. This fixed amount gives the unlimited right to drive in that section (box 2). On the other hand, there may be a kilometrage-dependent charge within the area (box 1).

Road-section based

Payment on the basis of road sections used is divided into:

-- Cordon systems (charge for passing the stretch of road that is part of the cordon);
-- Payment per stretch of road.

In cordon systems the charge is levied for passing the cordon (e.g. the Oslo toll ring). A route-oriented system is, for instance, the toll system in France. The more stretches of road used, the higher the charge. In both cases a subdivision is possible taking into account the (shadow) kilometrage of the stretches of road (boxes 3 and 5) versus a flat fare for passing stretches of road (boxes 4 and 6).

2.3. Examples

Figure 2 and the analyses in 2.2. are rather theoretical. In this section some existing charging systems will be located in the figure.

Fuel tax:	Usage-related, related to total trip, based on total number of kilometres[5] (in Figure 2, box 7).
Tunnel toll:	Usage-related, part of the trip, section-based, route, passing (box 6 in Figure 2).
System of toll roads, e.g. France:	Usage-related, section-based, route, number kms per stretch of road used (box 5).
Toll ring in Oslo:	Usage-related, part of the trip, section-based, based on passing the cordon[6] (box 4).
Singapore *vignette* system:	Usage-related, part of trip, area-based, unlimited (box 2).

2.4. Effectiveness of charging

In principle two effects may be expected from charging systems. These are generation of revenue and the modification of behaviour of car users. Of course, when the only goal of charging is to generate funds a behavioural effect is undesired and may even be counter-productive. In this paragraph the relation between the charging system and the effectiveness as far as modification of behaviour is pursued will be given. The golden rule for this relation is that the closer the charge is bound to the usage of the car/infrastructure the greater the behavioural effect will be. Next to that there is the factor of the avoidability of the charge. When, for instance, charging for urban infrastructure is combined with parking facilities at the edge of the urban area and adequate public transport from the parking to the urban area, the charge can be avoided by parking and using public transport, while the effect of the charge -- lesser car usage in the urban area -- is reached. The last factor is the level of the charge. To make things comparable, the level of charge is presumed here to be constant.

In the relation of charge and (behavioural) effect three elements can be distinguished:

-- The moment of payment (the closer the relation between usage and payment, the greater the effect);
-- The basis of the charge (a fixed tariff is less effective than a kilometre-based tariff);
-- The smallest unit which is charged (the smaller the individual stretches of road for which payment is obliged, the greater the effect [avoidability]).

In Figure 3 the three elements are combined. The percentages in the figure indicate the relative effect of such a charging system on behaviour. The most effective charge (direct, section- and kilometre-based) is put on 100 per cent. The figure indicates the effects. There is no underlying proof for the figures, they are the author's estimates. The practical effect will depend to a large extent on the exact form of charging and the context of both measure and available transportation system.

From the figure is will be clear that it is the author's opinion that direct charging (with balance in the car) is over 50 per cent more effective than raising the price of fuel (100 per cent versus 60 per cent) and that subscription for using all roads in an area is least effective (10 per cent).

3. TECHNICAL SYSTEMS FOR CHARGING ON URBAN INFRASTRUCTURE

3.1. Introduction

In Chapter 2 an overview of charging systems is given. This chapter lists and discusses the possible technical systems that can be used for charging. Here, only usage-related charging systems are addressed. Non usage-related charging systems are basically administrative systems; technical systems can support the administrative procedures.

3.2. Usage-related charging

Technical systems for usage related charging can be grouped into five families:

-- "*Vignette*" systems (fixed charge for a fixed period of time and area);
-- Taxation on fuel;
-- Manual charging/coin machines;
-- Automatic debiting;
-- Meters in cars.

3.2.1. Vignette systems

These systems let the user pay a fixed amount of money for the unlimited use of (urban) infrastructure during the period of validity of the *vignette*. The relation with usage is as follows: anyone who has to use the infrastructure has to pay; anyone who can avoid using the infrastructure does not have to pay. *Vignettes* are generally bought direct in advance of usage or have the form of subscriptions. Of course the relation between usage and payment is somewhat rude. Tailoring the *vignette* system (shorter period, smaller area; e.g. Singapore CBD) can improve this relation.

The technical forms the *vignette* system can take are:

-- Paper *vignette* to be displayed at the windscreen;
-- Automatic readable *vignette* at windscreen/car;
-- *Vignette* coupled to the registration number of the car.

Paper vignettes

In Singapore a system with paper *vignettes* is in operation. Ticket inspectors check whether cars driving in the "*vignette* area" carry the obligatory *vignette*. Enforcement is done by writing down the registration number of cars not carrying a *vignette*. Typically such a system can be used for small areas/limited numbers of roads, where cars drive with reduced speeds.

Automatic readable vignettes

Automatic readable *vignettes* are a natural extension of the paper *vignettes*. The enforcement task becomes easier because of automatic readings. One might think of bar code scanning as the technical system here.

Vignette systems coupled to the registration number

Vignette systems coupled to the registration number can be as follows. The car user buys a *vignette* for a certain number plate. All number plates for which *vignettes* are bought are registered in a computer file. In the *vignette* area a random recording is made of the number plates of cars using the infrastructure. The recorded number plates are matched with the computer file containing information for which number plate a *vignette* is bought. If no *vignette* appears to be bought the enforcement comes into action; the owner of the car gets a balance payable.

In the Annex, more details are given of the peak charging system that is under development in the Netherlands at the moment and which uses the technical system of number plate *vignettes* mentioned.

3.2.2.   Taxation on fuel

In all European countries excise on fuel is charged. By raising the excise or by introducing a new charge on the fuel price, charging for the use of urban infrastructure can be introduced. Taxation on fuel is a fair system. There is a close link between the user costs in such a system and the usage of infrastructure. Another great advantage of such a system is the low cost of introducing such a charge. For there is already a system to collect and hand over the excise revenue to the authorities. Extra taxation on fuel in urban areas is in particular applicable for isolated urban areas. In such a situation it is not possible to avoid the taxation by simply filling up outside the urban area where the charge does not apply. If it is easy to avoid the extra charge by filling up just outside the urban area, much of the effects (both in behaviour and in revenue) will be lost.

72

3.2.3.   Manual charging/coin machines

In this system the traffic is brought to a (near) stop at charging sites to hand over the amount of the charge. This is the traditional form of tolling, payment to cashiers or coin machines. The great problem in using these systems in urban areas is the small throughput per lane. Because of the small throughput per lane many parallel lanes are needed to guarantee a reasonable total throughput. In urban areas typically no space is available to build large toll plazas. In the remainder of this contribution no more attention will therefore be given to this technical system. The more so because the operational characteristics are well known.

3.2.4.   Automatic debiting

Under this heading a family of systems exists with the characteristic that the system consists of two parts; one in the car (on-board equipment, OBE) and one alongside the road (beacon),   between which parts there is a wireless communication.

Beacons are placed at locations where the charge is levied/settled. At the site of the beacon there is a form of communication between beacon and equipment in the car. The goal of this communication is to guarantee/verify the payment. If the transaction fails the enforcement is activated.

Types of payment

There are three types of payment with automatic debiting systems (ADS):

-- Pre-payment; the user pays before the use of the service;
-- Post-payment; the user pays after the use of the service;
-- Immediate payment; the user pays at the time of the use of the service.

In practice, the first type means that an account at the disposal of the charging organisation is opened, a certain amount of money is transferred to this account and when passing the charging point the account is debited with the amount due. The pre-payment can take the form of a subscription for a certain period of time, where at passing the charging point a verification takes place to check whether the subscription is valid. A last form of pre-payment is the situation where (real) money is transferred to a smart-card (electronic money) that is held inside the car and where the electronic account is debited at passage.

Post-payment means that some sort of bill is produced, based on the information that is communicated during passage of the charging point. The bill is sent to the owner of the OBE, who has to pay the bill later on.

Location of account

Furthermore, there is a distinction between the location of the account. The account may be located:

-- On board, held in the vehicle under the control of the user;
-- Centrally, held in ground equipment under the control of the charging organisation.

Tariff setting

ADS can also be marked off by the characteristics of the way the tariff is set. Is there a relation of the tariff with user/vehicle characteristics? Is there a payment per period/per passage? Are there any discount options?

Implementation

One-way ADS

The simplest form of automatic debiting is where only the identification of the OBE is being "transmitted" to the beacon. Based on the identification received, a bill is produced and sent to the owner of the identification (post-payment) or the charge is passed to the debit of a pre-paid account for this identification. Typically, after the beacon receives the identification a direct check is made using a black list containing all non-valid identifications. In case of a non-valid identification or no identification at all, the enforcement starts. The communication is one-way only. Technical forms are reading out bar-code stickers or electronic tags. Electronic tags are used in many places in the world, e.g. at the toll ring in Oslo.

Two-way ADS

Extra complications are introduced with two-way communication systems. The first version that will be described here does not have an on-board account. The two-way communication is used to store information in the OBE that is needed for the calculation of the charge. These systems are used at so-called "closed toll systems", being systems where the charge is calculated given the entrance point in the system and the exit point[7]. In automatic debiting systems the code of the entry point is communicated to the vehicle and stored in the on-board equipment. At the point of exit the beacon asks the OBE its identification and the information of the entry point; the entrance code is given by the OBE and the identification is verified and the amount of the charge is calculated[8]. Again, either a bill is sent to the owner of the identification or the centrally located account of this identification is debited.

Other two-way systems carry the balance in the car (as electronic money). At the charging site there is a communication between the car and the beacon and during the passage a certain amount of money is subtracted from the balance in the car. Such a system can be used with full anonymity. Also, the car driver is confronted immediately and directly with the cost of driving.

It is expected that such a direct confrontation with costs leads to the greatest behavioural effects of charging. If the transaction fails or if the amount of electronic money available is short, the enforcement comes into action.

Two-way ADS are under development/in the prototype phase.

3.2.5. Meters in cars

Another family of technical systems may be (odo)meters in cars. These meters register the usage of the car (kilometrage, speed, time of driving, parking, etc.). Reading of the meters should be done regularly (when filling up, during car examinations and so on), after which a bill can be produced. Such a meter system can be combined with a balance inside the car and direct settlement.

In the author's view, systems with meters in the car are very promising. Meters should be an integral part of the next generation's car usage. Meters will not only be used to monitor the condition of the car, but also for registration of behaviour for safety reasons (black box as in aeroplanes), for supplying optimal information on the condition of the roads to the driver, to protect cars from theft and abuse and last but not least to charge the user for the actual use of the infrastructure. It is clear that some of the meters' functions are regarded as positive by society, while others are considered as negative -- intrusion of privacy, extra taxes and so on.

In the author's view, initiatives for this type of meter should be taken by the car manufacturers and the meters should be introduced emphasizing the positive functions. Later on the other functions should be added. Such initiatives by the manufacturers will be unavoidable if the car industry is to enjoy another great future. If these initiatives are not taken, the disadvantages of the current car system will become uncontrollable and the car system will deteriorate! The author does not expect large-scale metering opportunities before the year 2010. For this reason metering is not taken into consideration in the remainder of this contribution.

3.3. Available technical systems for charging for the use of urban infrastructure

To conclude Chapter 3, the available technical systems to charge in relation to the usage of infrastructure will be summed up. The relevant systems are:

-- *Vignette* systems;
-- Taxation on fuel;
-- Automatic Debiting Systems (ADS).

4. CHARGING SYSTEMS FOR THE USE OF URBAN INFRASTRUCTURE

4.1. Introduction

In this chapter the results of the confrontation of objectives of charging (Chapter 1) and technical systems (Chapter 3) will be given. Preferential systems in relation to the objective will be identified and annotated.

Furthermore, remarks on operational aspects of the systems will be made to ensure the feasibility of the proposed systems.

Again, no attention is paid to charges that are not usage related, such as raising the annual car tax, taxation on the purchase of cars and other fixed charges and local taxes as mentioned in paragraph 2.2. Nevertheless one has to bear in mind that in the case where the only purpose of the charge is to generate funds, the indicated non usage-related systems may be very appropriate and cheap to use. Advantages are low operational costs and easy enforcement, because in most cases existing financial/administrative/enforcement systems can be used.

4.2. Preferred charging system in relation to the objective of charging

In Figure 4 the possible objectives of charging are listed as row entries. Column entries display the technical systems. The cells give an appraisal of the usability of the technical system for this objective. Criteria for the appreciation are whether the technical system can be tailored to the functionality needed, whether the effects of the technical system are in line with the objectives and the simplicity within the group of adequate systems.

From the figure it can be learned that the preferred system for charging in case of the wish for improving accessibility by temporal and spatial reduction of car usage is an automatic debiting system with balance in the car. As back-up, a system with *vignettes* is indicated; such a *vignette* should be very time and place specific (e.g. as in Singapore).

For charging tolls the preferred technical system is a simple, one-way, automatic debiting system.

In the case where the goal of the charging is to generate funds the preferred options are raising the price of fuel or introducing a *vignette* system for the urban area.

Where the objective is keeping down the environmental burden by reduction of the overall level of car usage, the preferred system is to raise the price of fuel. The back-up option is an ADS system with balance in the car. The extra complication of the back-up system is great. So raising the fuel price is the strongly preferred option here.

4.3. Operational aspects

Raising the fuel price

No special operational aspects can be found when raising the price of fuel.

Vignettes

In the *vignette* system care has to be taken that occasional users can easily take part in the system (easy to understand; adequate spread of selling points, etc.).

In the case where an ADS system is used there are a number of problems to be solved. The most important are related to:

-- Occasional users;
-- Privacy;
-- Enforcement.

4.3.1. Occasional users (vignettes and ADS)

Taking part in an ADS system requires having on-board equipment. Some users of the infrastructure where the ADS system is installed will be very occasional users, they may be confronted with the system less than twice a year. A decision has to be taken as to what to do with these customers. Are they required to take part in the ADS system? Will there be special arrangements?

In Oslo, the ADS system is combined with traditional toll booths for occasional users. As the majority of users passes with ADS, the magnitude of the toll plaza needed is very modest. In many cases such toll plazas can be fitted within the existing road space. Another possibility may be to have ticket machines for occasional users, where they can buy some kind of pass for using the roads for a certain period of time. These passes can be based on the number plate of the car (see Annex). When the number plate appears in the enforcement process it can be skipped on the basis of the information from the ticket vending machines.

4.3.2. Privacy

The ADS system with balance in the car does not require any information on the user or vehicle to be registered outside the car. So the user has permanent possession of all the information and abuse is not possible without his/her knowledge. Such an ADS system is by its nature privacy-friendly.

Privacy may be felt to be a problem with ADS systems without a balance in the car. In those systems the identification of the OBE is registered by a central computer system and people may fear abuse of this information [3].

The privacy aspect may be tackled by allowing anonymous accounts (number accounts). In that case the OBE is coupled with an account number instead of with a person. The user -- who is not known at the organisation -- has to ensure a positive balance on this account. When passing the charging site the charge is subtracted from the balance. In such a system the organisation does not know the identity of the user of a certain OBE identification This has the setback that the organisation is not able to warn the user in case of poor performance of his/her ADS system in the case of a low balance nor is able to give any information on the (mis)use of the OBE. Consequently, in exchange for absolute anonymity the user must accept greater own responsibility and risk for the functioning of the system.

4.3.3.   Enforcement

The enforcement will be activated after an unsuccessful communication between the equipment in the car and the road-side beacon. When it is clear that no guarantee for payment for the passage will be established there are two options:

-- Stop the car, or
-- Register the number plate of the car.

The choice between the options will depend on the local situation. If stopping the car causes a blockage for the whole traffic flow it is not an attractive option. Furthermore, the violator must be quickly dealt with, either by supplying a "help button" to connect the violator to a help desk or by manual action (which requires staff near the charging site).

On the other hand, using number plate information is only possible if the operator of the ADS system may use number plate information for enforcement and has access to the files with number plate data. Private companies levying tolls via ADS can be confronted with the impossibility of using number plate information for enforcement. In some countries or states it may be prohibited to use number plate files for tracking down the owner of the vehicle.

The ADS system in Oslo (Norway) can and may use number plate readings as proof for non-payment and does so. The Telepass system in Italy has chosen to stop cars if regular payment by ADS is not made.

Multi-lane enforcement

An important issue in enforcement is whether or not the ADS system has to operate in a full multi-lane environment. Multi-lane charging seems to have no problems any more, but multi-lane enforcement does. Here the problem is to photograph one and only one car in the full width of the road (which may have four lanes) when the charging system finds "a" non-payer. This non-payer can

79

be at any place in the width of the road. And given the anonymity of the charging process there is no further information on any of the cars in the photograph. A coupling with the information from the charging process is needed to be able to select for enforcement the one car that did not pay. In the Netherlands a prototype for multi-lane enforcement is produced by Rietschoten & Houwens/Philips [4]. The system uses vision techniques to do the job.

Without a multi-lane enforcement system the operator will be obliged to prevent car drivers from changing lanes near the charging site, but unless this is forced by barrier (reducing the throughput!) the system can still be cheated by drivers changing lanes, driving close to other vehicles, etc.

4.4. Conclusion

With all four objectives for charging for the use of urban infrastructure, adequate technical systems are available.

The confrontation of objectives and available systems leads to combinations of preferred options, as follows:

    i) Improving accessibility by reduction of car usage tied to time and place by two-way ADS systems with balance in the car;

    ii) Charging tolls by simple ADS systems;

    iii) Generating funds by raising fixed costs, introducing vignettes or taxation on fuel;

    iv) Keeping down the environmental burden by reduction of the overall level of car usage by raising the price of fuel.

Solutions for operational problems related to ADS (and *vignette* systems) are given.

5. SYSTEM REQUIREMENTS

5.1. Introduction

Typically, system requirements can be divided into:

-- Functional requirements;
-- User requirements;
-- Manager requirements;
-- Special requirements;
-- Limiting conditions and circumstances.

In the remainder of this chapter, typical requirements for charging in urban areas will be mentioned and analysed.

5.2. Functional requirements

The functional requirements are dictated by the objectives to be reached. In an earlier paragraph four objectives of charging in urban areas were distinguished:

-- Improving accessibility by reduction of car usage at peak periods;
-- Toll levying/parking fees;
-- Generation of funds;
-- Keeping down the environmental burden by reduction of overall level of car usage.

5.3. User requirements

-- *Occasional passers-by:*

Occasional passers-by, who never or hardly ever get to the urban area in which the charging takes place, should be able to participate in the system in a simple manner (cheap, little time, little orientation).

This is a demanding requirement especially for charging in urban areas. More attention to this point is given in sub-paragraph 4.3.1.

-- *Reliability:*

In regard to this requirement, the relation between the user and the charging body is essential. If this relation is according to civil law (for instance, in case of a toll road company) the reliability item can be dealt with in the contract between partners, which is being "negotiated" between the supplier and his client. If, on the other hand, the relation is according to public law (in case of charging in the form of taxation), usually no restriction on the rights of the public can be made. This means that in this latter case the reliability should be at a higher level.

The functioning of the system should be such that the chance to receive an unjust retrospective billing, due to the improper functioning of the installation, is acceptable.

-- *Vandalism:*

Provisions should be made to protect the equipment against substantial mechanical and electronic tampering to prevent problems for users caused by non-functioning equipment due to vandalism.

-- *Compatibility:*

If the user is confronted with charging systems in several areas compatibility of systems is desirable.

-- *Other user requirements:*

Driving conditions, privacy, user-friendliness.

5.4. Manager requirements

-- *Road capacity of the system:*

The charging system must be able to function in every possible combination of road design and traffic volume. This means that the amount of vehicles per time unit may not form a determining factor in the system.

-- *Occupied space:*

The construction of the system may not lead to occupying more space than is available at the existing road (network).

-- *Transit speed:*

The charging system must be able to function at speeds as required.

These three manager requirements apply especially in urban areas. The requirements are amongst the most severe.

-- *Enforcement:*

The enforcement system, as part of the enforcement strategy, should be set up in such a way that:

•   The level of enforcement must be greater than or equal to ..... per cent;
•   A passer-by should have a more than ..... per cent chance to receive a bill in case of an illegal passing.

The requirement on this point is especially severe on multi-lane roads. See sub-paragraph 4.3.3.

-- *Reliability:*

(See remark at user requirements)

The chance to encounter a faulty working of the system which results in an improper billing must be remote so that claiming of traffic fees with a normal functioning of the system leads to success, based merely on the convincing evidence produced by the user.

-- *Interoperability:*

In the case where several charging systems are used in neighbouring areas these systems should preferably be interoperable.

-- *Other manager requirements:*

Fraud protection, expansion flexibility, transaction capacity of the system, traffic (un)safety.

5.5. Special requirements

-- *Introduction requirements:*

In the case of electronic charging systems, the time to produce and fit the required number of systems should carefully be taken into consideration.

5.6. Limiting conditions and circumstances

-- *European developments:*

European developments in the field of standardization of informatics and telecommunication for road traffic are ongoing. The choice of charging system should as much as possible take into account these developments.

-- *Current legislation/legal provisions:*

The charging system must be legitimated.

-- *European issuing of rules/guidelines:*

The system must stay within the European issuing of rules and guidelines.

6. EUROPEAN STANDARDIZATION OF AUTOMATIC DEBITING SYSTEMS (ADS)

6.1. Introduction

In Europe several toll operators want to introduce ADS systems to upgrade the process of toll paying. Introducing ADS means time gains for the clients, smaller toll plazas, less cash money at the plazas, better working conditions and so on. Next to that there is a large potential for ADS to regulate traffic in different urban areas in Europe. The fact that ADS systems can be used for both tolling and for regulating traffic and given the possible spread of the systems over Europe, there is a wish to make these systems:

-- Compatible from a user's point of view (to be able to use the same on-board equipment in every European country);
-- Interoperable from an operator's point of view [to be able to direct the collected money (in different currencies) to the rightful claimant];
-- Compatible from a producer's point of view (to reduce the development budget per sold system, to create a competitive power through a standardized European market and to achieve exchangeability of parts and second sourcing of equipment).

6.2. Who is involved in the standardization process?

Worldwide: Standardization in IT and specifically in payment in transport is, worldwide, performed by ISO (International Organization for Standardization) and by IEC (International Electrotechnical Commission). Several standards which can be considered to be building blocks for payment in transport have in the past already been produced (e.g. ISO 7812, ISO 7816-1 to -3, etc.).

Europe: On a European level, standardization in the field is performed by CEN (*Comité Européen de Normalisation*). No actual standards, related to payment in transport, have been produced as yet. Specifically, the following Technical Committees (TC) relate to payment in transport:

-- CEN TC 224 "Machine Readable Cards, related Device Interfaces and Operations";
-- CEN TC 278 "Road Traffic and Transport Telematics".

Input: Implementation of advanced payment methods requires well thought-through input. Such input can originate directly from industry, authorities, universities, etc., including any related national development schemes. Examples of national schemes are, for instance, the Dutch *"Rekening Rijden"* project, the "VITA" project of the Spanish, Italian and French toll motorway companies, the Italian "Telepass" system for automatic toll collection and the French "PME" and Danish "Danmønt" generic payment methods project. Input can also be concentrated through broader research and development schemes, here in particular the European DRIVE programme.

6.3. The CASH project

One of the projects of the EC programme DRIVE II (Dedicated Road Infrastructure for Vehicle safety in Europe) (1992-94) is the project called CASH [Co-ordinating of Activities for the Standardization of HADES (High-level Automatic Debiting European system Specification)].

The primary task of CASH is the development and validation of standards in the field of ADS. This is done by drawing up the HADES specification; only specifying those requirements that are necessary for achieving compatibility and interoperability between ADS's, while allowing individual operators as much freedom as possible. This compatibility allows vehicles that are equipped with standardized On-Board Equipment (OBE) to travel from one operator's concession area to another and use a multitude of services offered by all operators who adopted systems based on the European standards.

CASH is a project of toll road operators in Austria, France, Italy and Spain and road administrations of the Netherlands, Norway and Sweden and the University of Newcastle (UK).

Figure 5 (taken from [5]) shows the possible services where an ADS system might be used. The matrix in the figure is a combination of type of infrastructure and tariffing principle. The shaded entries in the matrix mean that a possible service is recognised.

The scope of CASH in the first instance is to deal with combinations of:

-- Infrastructure: bridge/tunnel, link, network, area;
-- Tariffing principle: passage and entry-exit.

Figure 6 shows the typical ADS System Functions. The function **purchase** handles all contractual and financial interactions with the users (establishes contractual relationship, handles financial transaction, provides transaction and balance reports).

Transaction handles the actual ADS transactions; it informs and guides road users approaching an ADS station, checks authorisation of the user and collects the information that is needed for the calculation of the obliged fee (user characteristics, fixed and variable vehicle characteristics). The function **settling** recovers the service fee from the user's account. Therefore it calculates the obliged fee, recovers the fee from the user's account and records the transaction in a transaction report. The system function **enforcement** is responsible for detecting and recording road users, who have not fulfilled their financial obligations.

Next to the four functions in the figure, the function **clearing** also exists. Clearing is the function that takes information from the transaction reports and the financial transactions and sends flows of money from operators (that have received money) to operators (that have provided the service).

Cash takes into account the options of **pre-payment, post-payment** (and implicitly immediate payment) and of **on-board account and central account**; of **payment per period** and **payment per transaction** and **discount options**.

Operational constraints have been specified.

6.4. Developing standards

Insights with regard to those requirements that have to be standardized to be able to build compatible and interoperable systems, will be presented to the European standardization bodies, to be precise, Technical Committee 278 (TC) of the Centre for European Normalisation. The TC 278 will propose the actual standards. And based on these standards the industry will prepare ADS systems for the market.

So far, for the vehicle-to-roadside communication, the following standards and agreements already exist:

-- CEPT frequency allocation, decision by CEPT (European Conference of Postal and Telecommunications Administrations) to allocate bandwidth

to Initial Systems within Road Transport Informatics in the band 5.795 - 5.805 GHz with 3dBW allowed power [February 1991 (CEPT)],
-- DRIVE SECFO Logical Link Control, agreement on the datalink layer, based on the framing structure of HDLC (SECFO OSI ").

Some standards related to payment in transport are:

-- ISO 7816 (physical characteristics, dimensions and contacts and the electronic signals and transmission protocols);
-- ISO 7812 (numbering system for issuer identifiers);
-- ISO 4217 (currencies).

7. CONCLUSIONS

In this report attention is given to the question of charging moving motor vehicles for the use of urban infrastructure.

Charging systems for the use of urban infrastructure should be based on the objectives of the charging.

In the report, four objectives have been formulated:

-- Improving accessibility by charging to reduce car usage specific in time and location;
-- Charging tolls for the use of roads (car parking);
-- Charging just to generate funds;
-- Keeping down the environmental burden by charging to reduce the overall level of car usage in urban areas (as an intermediate solution).

The main, available tariffing principles of charging in urban areas are:

-- Related to possession or acquiring of a vehicle;
-- Fixed price over a period of time for use of the road ("vignette" systems);
-- Charge based on fuel usage (taxation on fuel);
-- Charge based on actual road usage by automatic debiting systems (ADS).

The confrontation of objectives and available systems leads to combinations of preferred options, as follows:

-- *Improving accessibility by reduction of car usage tied to time and place by two-way ADS systems with balance in the car;*
-- *Charging tolls by simple ADS systems;*

-- *Generating funds by raising fixed costs, introducing vignettes or taxation on fuel;*
-- *Keeping down environmental burden by reduction of overall level of car usage by raising the price of fuel.*

Solutions are given for some potential problems related to the use of ADS systems, being:

-- Facilities for occasional users;
-- Multi-lane enforcement;
-- Privacy.

The (European) standardization of ADS systems is under way and is targeted towards standardizing those elements of ADS systems necessary to allow car drivers to travel from one operator's concession area to another and use a multitude of services, offered by all operators who adopted systems based on the European standards by carrying only one ADS-OBE (on-board equipment) (compatibility). Furthermore, this standardization is targeted on reaching interoperability between ADS's, while allowing individual operators as much freedom as possible.

Setting standards for European ADS enables industry to develop a competitive market for ADS, with lower equipment costs, and achieve exchangeability of parts supplied by other sources.

Standards will be based on developments in the field of ADS and will be proposed by Technical Committee 278 of the *Comité Européen de Normalisation*.

FIGURES

Figure 1. **The transport triangle**

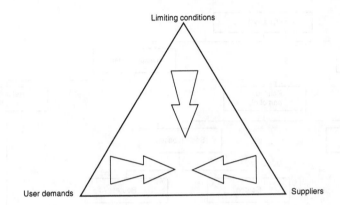

Figure 2. **Charging systems**

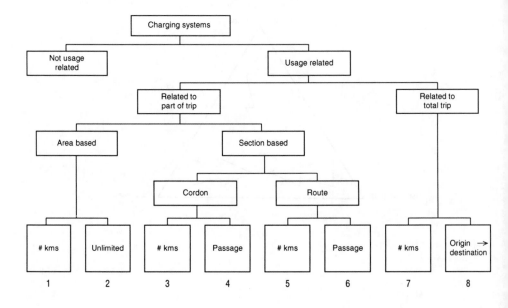

Figure 3. **Effects of the charging systems compared**

Basis of charging	Per **section** based on:		**Area** based on:	
Payment methods	kms	fixed	kms	fixed
Direct payment	100%	95%	85%	50%
Billing	60%*	40%	50%	25%
Subscription	25%	10%	20%	10%

(*) In the case where the basis for charging is known by the user during usage of the facility.

Figure 4. **Charging systems matrix**

CHARGING SYSTEMS OBJECTIVES	"vignettes"	Charge on fuel	Automatic Debiting systems		
			Only identification	Two way communication with off-car balance	Two way communication with on-car balance
Improving accessibility by reducing car usage temporal and spatial	back-up option note 1	inadequate	inadequate note 2		**preferred option** note 3
Charging tolls	inadequate	inadequate	**preferred option** note 4	not preferred option, less complicated option available (identification only) note 5	
Generate funds	**preferred option**	**preferred option**	not preferred, less costly options available		
Keeping down the environmental burden by reducing overall level of car usage (intermediate solution)	inadequate	**preferred option** note 6	inadequate note 2		back-up option, less complicated option available (fuel price)

note 1:   If the "vignette" is used very dedicated to place and time (Singapore, Randstad) the desired behavioural effect may be reached (see text).

note 2:   No direct confrontation of usage and costs: no (large) behavioural effect to be expected.

note 3:   Direct relation between usage and settlement; greatest behavioural effect may be expected.

note 4:   Solutions for occasional users needed; privacy can be overcome by numbered accounts (see text).

note 5:   Extended functionality of these forms of ADS not needed for simple toll levying.

note 6:   Not adequate when the high fuel price in the urban area can be avoided by filling up just outside the area; in that case the preferred option is the back-up option.

Figure 5. **Services matrix**

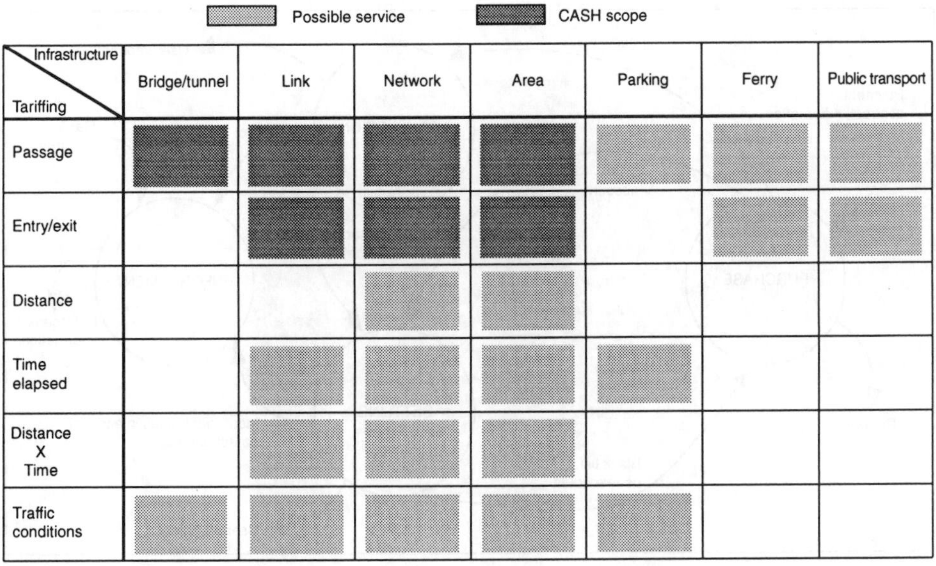

	Possible service			CASH scope		

Infrastructure / Tariffing	Bridge/tunnel	Link	Network	Area	Parking	Ferry	Public transport
Passage	CASH	CASH	CASH	CASH	Possible	Possible	Possible
Entry/exit		CASH	CASH	CASH		Possible	Possible
Distance			Possible	Possible			
Time elapsed		Possible	Possible	Possible	Possible		
Distance X Time		Possible	Possible	Possible			
Traffic conditions	Possible	Possible	Possible	Possible	Possible		

97

Figure 6. **ADS system functions**

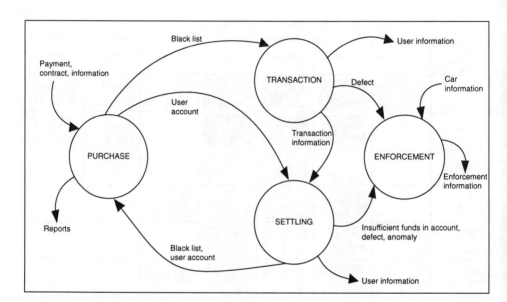

ANNEX

PEAK CHARGING SYSTEM IN THE NETHERLANDS

In the second half of the nineties a system of peak charging will be introduced on the network of main routes in the western part of the country (the Randstad; the area between Amsterdam, Rotterdam, The Hague and Utrecht). The area is heavily urbanised.

Payment of the peak charge will be obligatory between 06.00 and 10.00 in the morning. The effect will be a shift towards car pooling (sharing the costs) and driving after 10 o'clock and will result in a decrease of congestion (lost hours due to traffic jams and slow moving traffic) by one-third (33 per cent) during peak hours. Accessibility becomes much better with the introduction of the peak charging system.

The peak charge is related to the registration number of the car. Car users pay the charge for a certain registration number.

Car users can phone a free number to arrange payment. The user will be connected to a Voice Processing System (VPS). The computer system will ask the user to dial his or her account number and personal identification number. The computer then checks the position on the balance of the client/arrangement with the bank. If the payment is guaranteed, the peak charge is arranged and the result is positively communicated to the user.

Other users may prefer payment at a ticket machine. They type in their registration number and pay the charge. The ticket that is supplied is the proof of payment. Of all cars entering the network of main roads, one in six is photographed. The registration number on the photo is compared with the computer (white) list of number plates for which payment has been arranged. If no payment is registered, enforcement will come into action; a ticket with an extra charge will be sent to the owner of the car.

This system is regarded as intermediate until systems of automatic debiting and full multi-lane enforcement are operational.

The system will have a capacity of 130-200 million transactions per year.

NOTES

1. This conclusion might not be valid in developing countries.

2. High density "car-trains" are more appropriate for intercity trips.

3. In newly-built cities, car-free areas can be designed in such a way that those areas can function well. An example is the Dutch city of Houten (near Utrecht). Of course, in the western world 90 per cent of the future built-up urban area already exists and that fact also limits the applicability of taking physical measures.

4. On the other hand, these costs may be seen as subsidies to the activities located "around the infrastructure". Charging activities for these costs take the form of taxation in relation to the number of people attracted per year, the area in use, etc.

5. And related to the fuel efficiency of the car.

6. Tariff is the same at all cordon points.

7. Typically the user gets a ticket at the entrance; the ticket is handed over at the exit and there a calculation of the amount due is made.

8. Of course, storing the information of the entrance point can also be done in the central computer system. Considerations of privacy may lead to the wish to not store this information centrally.

REFERENCES

[1] *Second Transport Structure Plan*, Part D Governmental Decision, Ministry of Transport and Public Works, The Hague, 1990.

[2] *De Tolring in Oslo*, Trygve Solheim, Transport Economic Institute, Oslo, 1992.

[3] *Electronic Road Pricing: An idea whose time may never come*, Sandford F. Borins, York University, in *Transportation Research A*, 22a, No. 1, pp. 37-44, 1988.

[4] *The Kever System*, W.J. van den Bosch and K.C.J. Wijbrans, Rietschoten & Houwens Technology B.V., 1993 forthcoming in IEEE(?)

[5] *Description of the Automatic Debiting System*, DRIVE-CASH, September 16, 1992, Revision Date: May 3, 1993.

UNITED KINGDOM

David BANISTER
Planning and Development Research Centre
The Bartlett, University College London
London
United Kingdom

SUMMARY

London, May 1993

1. INTRODUCTION

The car symbolises the growth in mobility during the late twentieth century, and part of that philosophy has been the right to use that car wherever and whenever one wished. That right is now being questioned, with the increasing levels of congestion in urban areas, and the priorities for transport planning are now switching from increasing the capacity of the urban road transport system to ensuring that the interests of car owners are balanced with those of other people in cities. The car will remain the principal means of motorised transport, and the growth of car ownership and use is likely to increase over the next twenty years. The actual scale of increase is less clear. All across Europe (and elsewhere) fundamental changes are taking place in travel with the decline in importance of work based activities and the growth in social, shopping and leisure based activities.

Cities themselves are also changing. In the past they have operated as centres of physical production, but now they are becoming centres of information processing. Their primary function may be to produce and distribute knowledge and to control technology. The methods and processes of wealth creation are changing. Cities will now become much looser spatial organisations, as the costs of urban centrality and high land prices are balanced against the benefits of dispersal. The movement out of cities will continue with only front office functions remaining. Growth will be concentrated in corridors of good communications and at peripheral urban locations where it is cost effective to link in with both the transport and information networks. Interchanges may provide particularly suitable locations for logistical platforms, and international airports and major motorway intersections could provide the sites of maximum accessibility which would minimise location and transport costs.

The Group Transport 2000 Plus Report (1990) identified several common factors which contribute to congestion. First, there is a general deterioration in transport conditions due to inefficient use of the networks and the saturation of certain infrastructures (reducing the quality of all travel), and second there is a considerable nuisance caused by transport (including safety, quality of life, freedom of choice, social problems of mobility, environmental costs, and health effects). With the expected growth in Europe's economy over the next twenty years, these problems will worsen. This in turn will lead to a crisis of mobility and congestion.

Charging offers one of the main means by which the full costs of travel can be imposed on the user, particularly the car driver. It is not a new idea. Tolls were charged for many turnpike roads in Britain up to about 150 years ago, with the revenues being used to repay the costs of construction, maintenance and operation of the road. There was little control over them and it was in 1844 that the County Roads Boards were set up to supervise standards and charges. This paper presents the options for charging and the problems with implementation. The first half is descriptive in that the evidence is summarised leading to the conclusion that technically and theoretically the solutions to urban road congestion are clear, namely that prices should be raised and that prices should be directly related to the road conditions at the time the vehicle is being used. However, the real problems relate to implementation, and the second part of the paper is devoted to the politics of charging, equity and distributional issues, the questions of public acceptability of charges, and the links between charging and financing of the urban infrastructure. The focus is almost exclusively on the car with the arguments for and against charging as a means to reduce road congestion.

2. URBAN ROAD CONGESTION

Road congestion is one of the most popular topics of conversation as it occurs in all cities and major urban areas. Congestion causes economic loss, environmental degradation and a reduced quality of life, and the problems of congestion are likely to increase, given the expected growth in car ownership and incomes. There is no single solution to the problem and a package of measures need to be developed, appropriate to each particular situation and the perceived severity of the congestion. The Institution of Highways and Transportation (1992) identifies four main types of congestion:

-- Anticipated congestion:

  • related to bottlenecks and regular congestion which is due to physical limitations on capacity;

-- Occasional congestion:

  • related to seasonal demand and planned roadworks;

-- Exceptional congestion:

  • related to rare but predictable circumstances such as sports events;

-- Unexpected congestion:

  • related to accidents, breakdowns and adverse weather conditions.

Here we are concerned primarily with anticipated congestion in urban areas. The range of options available are considerable (see Table 1), and the focus of this paper is on those in the last category, namely restraining demand for car use through charging.

The consequences of congestion are substantial. The much quoted figure of the British Road Federation estimated that in 1985-86 congestion cost over £3 billion (at 1987-88 prices) in the seven largest UK conurbations, of which almost half was accounted for by London. In 1989, the Confederation of British Industry estimated that congestion cost the economy over £15 billion a year (3 per cent of GDP), of which nearly £10 billion occurred in London and the South East. Large concerns who have put detailed figures on the annual costs of London congestion to themselves include the Royal Mail letters (£10.4 million), Sainsbury (£3.4 million) and Marks and Spencer (£2.0 million) (London Boroughs Association, 1990). These figures include time delays, extra monetary costs for freight, lower productivity for commercial vehicles and drivers, and the increases in minor accidents and collision costs. These costs are rising in real terms by about 7 per cent per annum.

In addition to the economic costs of congestion, there are considerable environmental costs. Congestion reduces the efficiency of the transport systems and increases the consumption of energy. It creates an unpleasant environment for those living near to roads and direct links are now being drawn between traffic levels, emissions and the health of the population. Included here are the impact of lead on children's health and the rise in the incidence of asthma and bronchial related cases in polluted cities.

More generally, European Community policy has now clearly recognised the importance of sustainable mobility and it is moving towards charging for the infrastructure (CEC, 1992, paras. 345-346):

111

"Such a framework is the essential foundation for the realisation of the objective of sustainable mobility for the Community as a whole. If costs are not properly allocated, stresses are bound to arise as users favour disproportionately the transport services and systems that do not charge their full cost. If costs are being allocated on the basis of significantly different principles in different States or localities, not only will significant distortions affect competition between transport operators but it will be very difficult to develop Community-wide transport systems in a more integrated way. ... In the short term, emphasis will be placed on the development of a framework for the imputation of infrastructure costs. Particular attention will be given, in the light of the 1992 programme on the harmonisation of excise duty on diesel fuel, road tolls and charges to possibilities for adopting a truly territorial system for taxation of heavy goods vehicles. In the medium term, proposals will need to be made concerning charging for externalities so that environmental problems will be addressed by the fundamental economic mechanisms at work in the transport sector."

Although there has been opposition to a proposed EC carbon tax, there is a clear move towards increasing the charges for using the car. In the UK, the government is now committed (the Chancellor's Budget Statement, March 1993) to increase petrol prices in real terms by 3 per cent per annum, and this will give savings in CO_2 emissions of 1.5 million tonnes of carbon by 2000. There are further possibilities for increasing car use costs by switching the annual vehicle excise duty and insurance costs to an additional charge on petrol. These charges would be progressive in that the more the car was used, the greater the vehicle excise duty and insurance paid. However, although these charging strategies would switch costs to the use of the car rather than the ownership of the car, they are not directly related to whether the road conditions are congested or not.

3. ROAD PRICING

The idea that road user charges has its origins in the economics of Marshall (1890) who argued that, where unit costs increased as production rose, marginal costs would be higher than average costs. Pigou (1920) developed the general case for marginal cost pricing and Knight (1924) advocated congestion taxes to make more efficient use of road space. However, it was forty years later that road pricing developed as a practical policy for application in transport when the Smeed Committee (Ministry of Transport, 1964) linked these theoretical arguments to the technical feasibility. The possibility was rejected at that time

112

for technical, social and political reasons, even though the report concluded that Electronic Road Pricing was likely to be the most effective way of controlling urban traffic congestion. All of the theoretical and practical issues, concerning the means by which the external costs of transport can be internalised by levying a congestion charge, are comprehensively covered in the 80th ECMT Round Table (Goodwin and Jones, 1989). Table 2 outlines the four main methods of charging.

A plethora of publications have now been produced all arguing for some form of road pricing in London. The Institute for Public Policy Research (1989) suggested a daily charge of £3 to £4 which would be collected initially by an extra licence payment, but eventually through electronic road pricing (ERP) which would automatically debit sums from a Smart Card in the vehicle. This view is supported by the Chartered Institute of Transport (1992) which recommends the introduction of a timetabled programme for the introduction of ERP in London in the mid 1990s. Road pricing would form the heart of a policy package which would substantially ease the Capital's transport problems without major additional road construction and without massive demands on public funds. Their proposal is for the whole area within the M25 to be included, although much travel within this area would be free or charged at a low rate. It would cost £200 million to equip the vehicles, some £100 million to provide the charging infrastructure, and the annual running costs would be £70 million. The benefits would exceed £400 million a year and the revenues would amount to £600 million. The scale of investment required and the computing capacity for a road pricing scheme in London would be massive if all movements within the M25 were to be recorded or charged. The Smart Card technology is now available so that the vehicle entering the area would not have to stop, but the problems of setting up the roadside beacons and the electronic tags in the vehicles would take several years to be introduced, and this change would require primary legislation (Department of Transport, 1993). In the UK, two different forms of road pricing are being considered:

-- The Cambridge scheme has an on-vehicle meter which is triggered if the car's average speed falls below predetermined threshold levels. Payment is made through a Smart Card.
-- The Richmond scheme charges the vehicle for the amount of time they spend on roads inside the controlled area. The on-vehicle meter is activated by road side beacons at the edge of the zone.

Interest is also being shown within Europe as part of the EC DRIVE research programme where various technologies are being tested and compatibility standards are being set (CEC, 1991). Road user charges are seen as a means to raise money for new road construction (Norway), to regulate demand through price (UK) and to reduce traffic levels to achieve environmental improvements (Sweden). In the Netherlands, road user charges are being promoted for all three reasons above. Road user charges must be seen as part of a comprehensive package of transport and development measures to improve the overall quality of urban life, not merely another form of taxation. Motorists already feel that they pay too much. The actual form of charging could take several forms:

-- A charge could be levied for the use of a particular junction or link, such as on a toll road, but this option is unlikely in urban areas because of implications for traffic diversion.
-- A charge could be imposed to cross a cordon, either as a one way or two way toll. This system has been used in the Norwegian schemes.
-- A driver could purchase an area licence to enter the restricted area at particular times and there is no limit as to the total number of trips that could be made. Stockholm is proposing a scheme of this form.
-- Charges could be directly related to some measure of the vehicle's contribution to congestion, and this would take the form of a full electronic road pricing scheme (e.g. Cambridge).

Road pricing is equally appropriate to the road freight sector, and many of the arguments raised against road pricing for cars are less applicable (see Table 3). The quote in Chapter 2 from the EC White Paper on Transport Policy (CEC, 1992) suggests that in the short term it is the road freight sector that is likely to see changes in the charging systems. Harmonisation of vehicle excise duty is required and careful targeting is necessary to ensure charges can be related to distance and tonnage (or capacity). Higher charges in the road freight sector would ensure better vehicle utilisation, fairer competition between road and rail (and other modes), and raise the importance of transport costs as part of the total production and distribution process.

The purpose of marginal cost pricing of road space is to increase the costs of using the car in congested urban areas so that the full social costs are charged. This strategy is likely to result in a range of different responses (Adams, 1989).

-- A redistribution of trips among competing modes, from those that have become relatively or absolutely more expensive to those that have become cheaper, including car sharing and car pooling.
-- A redistribution of trips to different routes through the network, from routes which have become more expensive to those which have become cheaper.

114

-- A redistribution of trips over time, from those times of day which have become more expensive to those times of day which have become cheaper.

-- A redistribution of journeys to different destinations, from those that have become more expensive to reach to those that can be reached more cheaply.

-- A suppression or generation of trips depending on whether travel has become more expensive or cheaper.

The conclusion Adams (1989) reaches is that *"whether restraint is exercised by congestion or road pricing the short term effects will be similar -- a displacement of traffic and its externalities to other modes, other roads, other times, other places, and a suppression of some trips altogether."* The question now addressed is whether road pricing is the only means by which urban road congestion can be reduced.

4. ALTERNATIVES TO ROAD PRICING

There are many alternatives to road pricing and any city is likely to adopt a package of measures individually tailored to its own requirements (see Table 1) -- here we elaborate on three possibilities:

4.1. Parking alternatives

Parking policy is one strategy which has been accepted by the general public. It combines a strategy of restraint through the total numbers of spaces and the time permitted to stay, and a charge can be imposed which relates to each individual trip being made. However, several arguments have been raised against the effectiveness of parking policies. The most important in the UK is the lack of control over much of the parking spaces in many cities, as local authorities are only responsible for between 30-60 per cent of spaces. Secondly, where parking is scarce, priority is usually given to short term parking, but this may encourage more traffic into the area. Associated with this is the problem of congestion caused by vehicles searching for a parking space. Thirdly, parking does not reduce through traffic, and some have argued that this problem is insoluble for regulatory parking policies (Glazer and Niskanen, 1992). Finally, there is the problem of enforcement and illegal parking that often takes place when no spaces are available. Despite these limitations, parking is still likely to be the main means by which car use can be controlled.

A market priced parking strategy which involved appropriate enforcement measures and controls over all forms of city parking (both public and private parking) would ensure minimum parking time and full costs were imposed on users. These parking charges would be equivalent to the office rent and unified business rate level for the particular area. This would mean a doubling of existing hourly parking rates in Central London (Banister, 1989). Effective parking policy must include enforcement and payment of Fixed Penalty Notices together with the identification of frequent offenders. In addition, the removal of vehicles has acted as a major deterrent to illegal parking (NEDC, 1991). Parking charges in other cities and in the suburbs would be less that those in Central London, but in each case the same approach would be adopted, namely to relate charges directly to the local rental levels.

Appropriate pricing of parking is a simpler mechanism to allocate road space than a comprehensive road pricing scheme. It can be introduced immediately with on-street parking and publicly controlled off-street parking, but statutory powers would have to be acquired to take control of off-street private parking. Parking control and enforcement could either be privatised or given to the local authorities to operate. With the recent advances in technology, it is now possible to have prepaid parking cards which can be automatically read and recharged when necessary, thus reducing the twin problems of non payment and vandalism. Differential charges can be levied according to time of day or day of week, and preferential charges could be given to residents and disabled drivers. Parking controls offer an effective means to charge for road space when the vehicle is not in use. Cars on average are only used for between 48 and 72 minutes each day, depending on the day of the week. Over the week as a whole, the car is used for about one hour a day. The car is parked away from the home for between 5-6 hours a day.

Although parking policies may be second best alternatives to road pricing, they have the overriding advantage that they are already common-place in all cities. The extension of parking controls and the introduction of appropriate prices are likely to be more acceptable to the public. The main disadvantage with parking is that the price only relates to the location of the destination, the length of the stay, and the time of day. Road pricing would also include a charge for the trip length and the route followed. Many researchers argue for comprehensive parking strategies as the main means to charge motorists the full costs of using the urban infrastructure (e.g. Verhoef *et al.*, 1993; Small, 1992).

4.2. Technical alternatives

The current generation of traffic management systems allow complete interaction between the user and the system through real time information and on board computers. Traffic management schemes have been very effective in squeezing more capacity out of a given road network, and the expectation here is that technology can continue that process through intelligent highways and smart cars. Road users will be affected in three different ways:

--   Information services to the traveller which will allow decisions to be made on the basis of the best real time information. These services would apply equally to public transport services and to route guidance information given to the car driver.
--   Control systems within the vehicle. By the year 2000, it is estimated that 10-15 per cent of the costs of new cars will relate to Road Transport Informatics (RTI) services (Lex Motoring, 1992).
--   Control over the transport network, including demand management and traffic control systems.

RTI will also have considerable commercial applications through more efficient management of freight companies and public transport services.

This futuristic vision was apparent in two major European research programmes of DRIVE (Dedicated Road Infrastructure for Vehicle Safety in Europe) and PROMETHEUS (Programme for European Traffic with Highest Efficiency and Unprecedented Safety) where the twin objectives of increased efficiency and safety were set. More recently, new programmes have tested market applications in a series of European pilot projects, and with the parallel programmes in Japan (the Road Automobile Communication System and the Advanced Mobile Traffic Information and Communication System) and the USA (the Intelligent Vehicle Highway System), there is now an unstoppable impetus for the application of RTI to road transport (Kashima, 1989). Transport represents more than 6 per cent of GNP with more than 10 per cent of the average family budget being devoted to transport, and there is a strong expectation that with the growth in car traffic "*bottlenecks will inevitably occur in land infrastructure in Europe*" in the 1990s (CEC, 1991, p. 5).

To many people the opportunities offered by RTI must seem very attractive, but this technologically led top down approach to the problems of traffic congestion and network inefficiencies must also realise its limitations. In isolation, RTI will not solve these problems, and at best it may help to alleviate some of the particular instances of congestion, if combined with other transport and land use policies. The RTI technology is likely to exist in parallel with the old technology, its costs (at least in the short term) are likely to be considerably higher than existing technology, and market penetration will be limited (at least initially). Given these uncertainties, it is unclear whether RTI will actually have any impact, particularly where consumer choice is involved (Banister, 1992a). Its greatest potential would be in systems about which the consumer does not know (e.g. car engine management systems) and in business activities where there might be clear competitive advantages in using the technology. In both of these applications the car industry and the private sector can be expected to take the lead. There may be a role for information services to develop as an industry in their own right. The EC is concerned over the power of the USA which accounts for over two-thirds of the world's electronic databases. It wishes to develop a common EC industry to increase the existing market share of the UK, France and Germany which between them account for just 13 per cent of the world total (Vogel and Rowlands, 1990).

The impact of RTI on transport congestion will be limited, at least in the next twenty years. The most effective forms of RTI will be those which improve traffic management (including public transport management). These passive systems require no action from the user of the system, but increase the reliability and efficiency of the system itself. The second area of significant potential is in logistics and in the organisation of production and distribution systems, principally in the road freight sector. Here, competitive principles can be applied to ensure the operational efficiency of companies is maintained, and RTI may form a crucial part of that competitive advantage.

Smart Cards with stored value would permit many of the present concessionary and promotional fares to be much more clearly targeted to the needs of individual users. Stored value cards could make users aware of the costs of each individual trip and there is a possibility that such a smart card could be available for all modes. The Confederation of British Industry (1992) has proposed the Ultimate Integrated Ticket (UIT) which can be used to pay for different transport services. It could be used to hire cars, for public transport, home delivery services and taxis. Part of the payment system could be prepaid, and another part could be credit or debit based. The aim would be to ensure maximum flexibility and full awareness by the user of the actual costs of using any particular mode.

Where most uncertainty occurs is in the user response to RTI, and how they may react to "Smart Vehicles". Diffusion of innovation takes time, the technology itself often changes rapidly, and access to the technology is limited by knowledge and price. A major barrier to the acceptance of RTI technology is consumer awareness, the knowledge base required, and the realisation of the full potential advantages that the technology must bring. Even if its full potential were achieved a supplementary question must be raised. Is there a physical limit to the capacity of the road network beyond which no further capacity can be squeezed? Restrictions will still have to be placed on the road user through pricing and regulations, despite all the technological advances.

4.3. Land use alternatives

Perhaps the most important contribution to reductions in congestion is to acknowledge the close links between land use and transport, and make a greater use of the planning system to control transport growth. The principal objective must be to maximise accessibility and minimise trip lengths. These twin policy objectives would guarantee the greatest levels of demand for public transport, cycling and walk modes. By ensuring the appropriate mixture of land uses, the availability of local facilities and employment, and good quality public transport, the greatest efficiency in levels of transport would be obtained and the levels of energy consumption per trip and per person would be minimised, even where trip generation rates are high. The environmental costs of transport would also be significantly reduced if the dependence on car travel was reduced and balanced communities were encouraged (Banister, 1992b).

Decisions here need to be made at the strategic level, but it is here that the planning system is weakest. The new system of Regional Planning Guidance (RPG) offers the opportunity for integration within each region, but it does not integrate between the Departments of the Environment and Transport. It is solely the responsibility of the Department of the Environment (ACC, 1991). Although Development Plans have been strengthened by the recent Planning and Compensation Act, Country Structure Plans are less important than they used to be, and Counties no longer have the co-ordination role for public transport. Too much responsibility for local policy on the land use transport interactions is given to the District Plans which are implementation plans, not strategic documents. A recent study by the County Surveyors' Society (para 9.18, quoted in ACC, 1991) showed that in 1989 over 10 000 applications which had important implications for highways were dealt with by District Planning Authorities.

In the recent draft Planning Policy Guidance (PPG) on Transport (Department of the Environment, 1993) the importance of the links between land use and transport have been recognised with the objective of providing accessibility, but "minimising transport costs in the widest sense, including costs to the environment" (para. 1.4). Congestion is seen as being both economically inefficient and environmentally damaging. Local authorities are now being required to explicitly consider locational policies in their development plans and *"the travel implications of all significant new developments should be considered carefully before planning permission is granted"* (para. 2.2).

In the Green Paper on the Urban Environment, the EC argues very strongly for a compact city as the solution to the problem of urban congestion, lower energy consumption and lower pollution levels, and for the improvement of the quality of life (CEC, 1990). It goes beyond the sole concern with environmental sustainability to cover the impacts on the natural environment and the quality of urban life, and its views the city as a resource which should be protected. The quality of life in European cities has deteriorated as a result of uncontrolled pressures on the environment and the spatial arrangement of urban areas which has led to urban sprawl and the spatial separation of functions. These factors have undermined the compact city which in turn has reduced creativity and the value of urban living. The return to the functionally mixed compact city is a solution, the only solution to these problems.

At present, when decisions are made on whether to approve new developments, traffic generation forms an important element but only on a project basis. Assessment of the traffic implications on the system as a whole for the complete range of individual projects does not take place. A comprehensive perspective would allow traffic impacts to be assessed on the plan and programme levels, not just on the individual project level. Transport is a key factor in influencing land use and development patterns and it is also linked closely with economic growth. All three options outlined above have an important role to play in reducing levels of demand and hence congestion. However, some form of road pricing may still be necessary, but there are several key problems of implementation. These are not theoretical or technical, but political.

5. THE POLITICS OF ROAD PRICING

Clear links have now been drawn between transport congestion, the environment and the quality of life. All the evidence leads to one conclusion, namely that cities must develop as attractive, safe places to live and they must provide affordable housing, employment opportunities for a range of skills, and provide a diversity of social and leisure opportunities. Policies can all operate in the same direction to improve the environment, increase efficiency and promote accessibility. Some of the pricing and charging options outlined in the previous two sections present the case for a combination of economic and planning levers, placed in a changing technological context. Traffic calming and pedestrianisation are seen by some as the only feasible solution to the problems created by the car (Tolley, 1990), as traffic limitation strategies attempt to slow traffic down, enhance safety and the quality of life in urban areas. It is not possible or desirable to continue to build roads to accommodate the expected growth in the demand for road traffic. Increases in capacity encourages more travel and longer trips, and reductions in capacity may encourage less travel and shorter trips. Promotion of co-ordinated public transport on exclusive rights of way (rail and bus routes) would provide fast, reliable and safe services and help change the traditional image of buses. In the UK, one of the main benefits from deregulation has been the growth in minibus operations. In 1985-86, minibuses and midibuses accounted for 14 per cent of the British bus and coach stock. By 1990-91, this figure had increased to over 27 per cent (19 700 vehicles). These smaller vehicles fill the gap between the taxi and the large bus, they allow hail and ride operations, they increase the feeling of a personalised service and they provide greater security to the traveller (Banister and Mackett, 1990). Flexible routing, shared taxis and the greater use of technology through passenger information systems can all increase the attractiveness of public transport. However, charging for cars in urban areas must still be seen as one of the major policy options available. But several important issues still have to be resolved, and three are covered here -- equity, public acceptance and boundary effects.

5.1. Equity issues

It is generally argued (e.g. IPPR, 1989 and Jones, 1992) that the low income car owners will suffer the greatest detrimental impact from road pricing, particularly if adequate public transport is not available. Non car owners may benefit from the increased reliability and greater productivity from public transport which can now operate under less congested conditions. Various levels of charging have been proposed for London, in the range £3-5 (IPPR, 1989) or £5 (NEDO, 1991), and it is calculated that peak hour traffic would fall by 9 per cent and off peak traffic by 18 per cent if charges were set at these levels. Conventionally, elasticities of demand are considered to be low, particularly in the short term, and substantial charges would be necessary to achieve the levels of traffic reduction required to have an impact on traffic flows (10-15 per cent: Goldstein, 1989). The standard arguments in favour of road pricing tend to ignore the distributional effects by concentrating on the benefits to society as a whole from congestion charging.

Analysis of the main national source of Family Expenditure information (Government Statistical Survey, 1992) suggests that charges on the levels proposed above would have a substantial impact on household budgets (Annex 1 presents the detailed figures). In 1992, the average household spent 15.4 per cent of their weekly expendable income on transport, split between motoring 13.2 per cent (half on net purchase of vehicles, spares and accessories; and half on maintenance and running costs) and public transport fares and other travel costs 2.2 per cent (including rail, bus and coach, air, other vehicles and boats, and other).

If it is assumed that a charge of £4 is made on an average journey within the road pricing area of London, this means that £20 per week is needed to pay for 5 journeys per week in the road priced area (this could be five work journeys or other journeys). On average, car owning households in London make 9.8 journey stages per week by car as a driver. There are seven alternative strategies which could be adopted (see Table 4), but it is not possible to assess from the Family Expenditure Survey exactly which package of alternatives would be used. However, some clear indications can be given if it is assumed that the driver enters the road pricing area. From National Family Expenditure Survey data:

-- No household income group spends £20 a week on public transport fares and other non motoring costs. On its own, it would not be possible to transfer monies within the household transport budget from public transport to car (Option 2).
-- For the lowest four income groups (Annex 1), the total budget spent by car owning households on motoring is less than £20 per week, so it would be impossible for these households to meet the road pricing charges from their existing transport budget.
-- For the next six income groups in households owning a car (Annex 1), the £20 charge would mean an increase of 60 per cent in the motoring budget.
-- Only in the top six income groups (Annex 1) would the impact of the £20 charge be less than a third of current motoring expenditure levels in car owning households.

It seems very unlikely that current motoring budgets in car owning households could be made to pay for road pricing charges which on average would come to about 40 per cent of the existing levels of motoring expenditure. Either the total household budget would have to be increased (Option 4), or changes in the internal distributions of budgets between the different expenditure heads would have to be made (Option 3). Expenditure on transport would increase from 19.4 per cent to 27.1 per cent of all household expenditure for car owning households, and for the five lowest income groups transport would account for over 30 per cent of household expenditure. Cutbacks would have to be made in other expenditure categories such as housing and food. Again, this is unlikely to be acceptable politically, so in the longer term higher wages would have to be paid to compensate for the charges, and this in turn would be both inflationary and reduce the intended impact of the road pricing. Alternatively, compensation could be paid through the taxation and benefits system or through subsidy. But this seems a cumbersome means to achieve the objective of marginal social cost pricing of road space. In London, some £1 000 per annum of additional income would be required to pay for the road pricing out of taxed income unless a third party is paying the charge (Option 5). The only option left to most households would be to change mode (Option 1), or to adapt the car journey (Option 6), or not to make the trip at all (Option 7). The Family Expenditure Survey is not a suitable data source for suggesting which of these alternative strategies is the most likely to be adopted.

The Family Expenditure Survey data simplifies the situation, yet the purpose of road pricing is to reduce the amount of travel by car, and changes on the levels suggested here are likely to have a very substantial impact on household travel patterns. However, there is an *impasse* -- between the assumed low elasticities of demand and the necessarily high levels of road pricing charges to achieve the desired reductions in travel; and the effects on household budgets of the required charge levels. In addition, it can be argued that the low income car owner will not be able to pay the charge at all, and so has no choice as to whether to enter the road pricing area. These low income car owners do not just include the poorest households in the UK, but all households on average income levels. For an average car owning household, £50 per week is spent on travel out of a total budget of £259 (19.4 per cent); to meet the £20 road pricing charge would increase the transport budget to 27.1 per cent or result in the existing budget being reduced by 40 per cent so that only the essential trips could be undertaken. This is the crucial problem for road pricing, namely whether it is politically acceptable -- about half of the motoring population would not be able to meet the levels of charges being discussed without making substantial changes in their activity, travel and mode choice decisions. It is not just a question of equity, but one of affordability.

5.2. Public acceptance

The report by the Harris Research Centre on Londoners' views to road user charges (NEDO, 1991) takes a sample of 489 Londoners and asks them a series of questions on transport, the quality of life and a range of possible charging options. Congestion is perceived as the most pressing problem for those living in London and rates higher than housing, crime and poor public services, but road user charges are not popular. Improvements to public transport, reduced fares and improved roads are all seen as more important. Less than half the sample (43 per cent) felt that road pricing was "acceptable to some degree". This acceptability rises to 62 per cent if the revenues from road user charges are used for public transport investments and for road improvements. In all the debate on pricing this issue comes through as being of paramount importance. To achieve any level of public acceptability, road pricing cannot be used merely to raise revenue for the Exchequer. The monies must be used for improvements in the transport system, particularly public transport. However, the notion of hypothecation is always likely to be resisted by the Treasury. Unless this impasse is resolved, ERP is unlikely to be publicly acceptable and hence it will be politically unpopular.

The respondents were invited to suggest their possible reactions to charging (see Table 5). This information is difficult to interpret as the situation is hypothetical and it is assumed that there is no constraint on budget. Equally, it is assumed that there will be no readjustment process as a result of seeing less car traffic on the road and a switch back to the car. It is also assumed that the public transport system can cope with the expected increase in demand. The conclusion that a charge of 50p per hour at peak times could reduce car trips in Central London by about one-quarter must be seen as optimistic. Questions which present unconstrained choices of hypothetical alternatives are not good predictors of actual behaviour.

The Harris survey is an important addition as it presents the views of the electorate. It illustrates the fact that transport congestion in London is now a crucial factor in reducing the quality of life, but it also illustrates the desperate situation. Suggestions made by the sample revolve around the improvement of public transport services. This is important and benefits public transport users, but does it make people leave their cars at home? Many of the respondents seemed to indicate that their company would pay for any charge and so they would benefit through faster speeds on the less congested roads. This factor may explain why the higher social groups were more in favour of road pricing. More worrying is the view of the young who seemed to be the most car oriented and the most vociferous in their opposition to road user charges. The political support of this group within the electorate is important.

The NEDO (1991) report has been highlighted, but it reflects much of the social research which has been carried out on road pricing in the UK (see Jones for a comprehensive review, 1992). There seem to be four basic reasons why residents are against road pricing.

-- The first relates to the problems of anonymity. This public concern was raised in the Hong Kong ERP Demonstration project and it has now been overcome with the development of systems which are designed to be non traceable. But as Buchan observes (1992, p. 10), it is important to separate automatic enforcement methods which may raise privacy issues from any infringements of privacy inherent in the road pricing technology.

-- The second reason is the fear over the technological driven future and the belief that the technology is fallible and will fail. It seems that passive systems about which the general public know little are less undesirable than systems about which they have discretion. Simple understandable systems are preferable and a substantial public information programme is desirable if public acceptability is to be assured. The time required for innovation diffusion and acceptance is considerable and can only take place at the level of the slowest participant if the system is to be comprehensive.

-- The third concern is the feeling that the revenues raised are just another form of taxation imposed on the motorist. Although all of the surveys carried out on public attitudes report strong negative responses to road pricing, that resentment is reduced if the monies raised are reinvested in the transport system. Jones (1991, p. 252) has carried out a comprehensive review of public attitudes to urban traffic problems and his conclusions were that:

  • We find the strongest support for policies that provide alternatives or supplements to car use, without directly affecting the ability to travel by car: park-and-ride schemes, public transport improvements, encouraging walking and cycling. Support for more road building is expressed by about half of the population, but this also has a sizeable proportion against as well as for. The introduction of some form of road pricing in inner or central city areas is generally supported only by a minority (typically a quarter to a third); and a general increase in petrol tax is regarded with least enthusiasm.

-- The final reason is a deep resistance to any interference with the individual's relationship with their car, in terms of its perceived status,

125

the privacy it offers, and the value to the individual. Jones (1993) calls this the "herd instinct", as economists see congestion and delay as an externality, yet drivers see it as something internal. There is a resentment against paying for something which is not wanted and something that has already been discounted in their travel decisions. There is more support for policies that affect all drivers equally (strengthening the cohesiveness of the clan) over policies (such as pricing and charges) which are seen as divisive.

5.3. Boundary effects

The scale of the road pricing scheme also has important implications for the economic viability of city centres. If the population perceives that there is an additional charge for bringing their car into the city centre, they may carry out their business elsewhere. This in turn would create pressures for development at peripheral or non-charged locations, and land values and rent levels in the city centre may have to be reduced to compensate for the potential loss. More dispersed patterns of activity will be more energy intensive as trip lengths are increased, and it becomes harder to provide a comprehensive public transport service where trip patterns are dispersed. Proponents of road pricing would argue that greater efficiency within the city centre would increase the productivity of firms and individuals, so that these benefits would outweigh the additional road charges made. This argument simplifies the position in at least three important respects. Will the road pricing system make a significant impact on operating costs or will the perception still remain that the price being paid is greater than the benefits being received by the individual and firm? Even if the economy of the city were to improve, would the overall efficiency and productivity of the regional economy as a whole also improve? The overall effect may be negative if congestion is redistributed from one location to another. This observation would argue for road pricing being introduced as part of a citywide and regional strategy where the overall impact of road pricing on the economy is assessed. Finally, many firms and individuals are making the decision to leave the city for a range of reasons, including congestion. These decisions are long term and once made are difficult to reverse. There seems to be little evidence of recentralisation of cities and the argument that road pricing could provide the trigger for a new generation of high density cities is unsubstantiated.

At the local level the technological solution to this problem is to have a "fuzzy road pricing system" as proposed in Cambridge, where the actual charging area would be flexible, depending on the prevailing level of congestion. Equally, charges could be varied so that not all locations would be charged at the same rate. Such a strategy, if applied consistently, would give signals to the market as to where businesses should be encouraged to locate. Economic theory has failed to determine the appropriate levels of charges which should be imposed, and it seems that a heuristic approach would be adopted. This is what Goldstein (1989, p. 16) calls a rational procedure -- "*road pricing an amount that yields the desired improvement.*" Flexible boundaries and flexible charges may help mitigate some of the problems inherent in road pricing, but it then raises other issues as to who should control the system, and how would it be made accountable and to whom. Evans (1992, p. 242) argues that there are perverse incentives for government as pricing may not take place according to the optimal price, but to the revenue needs of government. The monopoly over the supply of roads in urban areas means that prices would be higher than necessary and capacity would be undersupplied. He concludes that an independent body is needed to regulate prices. Bayliss (1992, p. 11) suggests that central government should be the enabling authority with local government taking on the role of sponsor and manager.

5.4. Conclusions

Road pricing has been seen as the major opportunity for charging users the full costs of using scarce urban infrastructure, and the economic arguments are clear. However, there are many other problems, three of which have been raised in this section, and each is sufficient to postpone implementation. Underlying all the problems is the question of whether a market for transport infrastructure exists in urban areas. Roads are seen as a public good and essential to being able to carry out ones activities. Access is at present rationed by time through congestion, so why not allocate space by price and willingness to pay. Would this solution lead to greater efficiency and equity?

Average cost pricing is used in most other sectors to allocate costs to users -- the closest analogy is with the telecommunications industry where one is charged a fixed cost for the equipment and a variable charge related to the time, distance and duration of the call. However, as with most utilities, there is not a real market as one supplier is in a virtual monopoly position (e.g. telecommunications, electricity and water). Prices are set at average levels and there is capacity in the system to absorb growth. With congested roads in urban areas there is no spare capacity and so the proposal is to create capacity through marginal cost pricing. It seems that the arguments being applied to road transport are unique as a different price structure is being proposed because there is a shortage of capacity. The response in the other sectors would be to create additional capacity rather than reduce consumption.

Even if pricing is accepted as the means to reduce consumption, then the scale of any increase is likely to be substantial if target levels of a 10-15 per cent reduction in traffic are to be achieved. Short run elasticities of demand are low (Goodwin and Jones, 1989). In affluent economies with high levels of car ownership, road pricing is likely to lead to substantial sums of money being raised. Some road users will be priced off the road and the additional capacity may give benefits to those drivers continuing to use the road system until a new congested equilibrium is reached. The marginal low income car owner will be the person to switch mode, destination, route, time or suppress the trip, whilst other users will pay the charge. As noted earlier, the suggested charges for entering Central London have been £3-5 per day. If a car is used for five journeys a week (half the current level) within the road priced area, then the total weekly cost would be £20 (or £1 000 per annum). Weekly household expenditure on motoring in Greater London (1992) is £32.60. If this is all spent in car owning households, then the increase in the cost of motoring would be about 40 per cent. Transport expenditure already accounts for 17.6 per cent of all household expenditure in car owning households in Greater London, and road pricing would increase this proportion to 23.5 per cent given the assumptions made here. The effect of such an increase is likely to be inflationary as Londoners attempt to recoup this cost in higher wages. More important though is the almost impossible task of trying to "sell" to the public the unspecified time savings which result from entering the road pricing area. It is likely that the costs substantially outweigh the perceived welfare benefits.

Congestion pricing and parking controls are "auto equalisers" designed to remove built in biases and subsidies (Cervero and Hall, 1989), but in themselves will not resolve the problem of urban congestion. Many of the problems of congestion relate to non-recurring incidents such as accidents, lane closures and unpredictable events (Chapter 2: Unexpected Congestion). In the USA, some 50 per cent of freeway congestion is caused by these types of incidents (Cervero and Hall, 1989). It is here that technology has a key role to play through driver information systems such as route guidance and variable messages. Continuous monitoring of roads allows emergency vehicles to reach incidents in the shortest possible time, it can help minimise the length of any delay and it can help slow down traffic and redirect if necessary. In the longer term, fully automated highways and small electric/hybrid city vehicles may replace the current generation of cars. These vehicles may be hired or leased rather than owned, and would complement other more traditional petrol/diesel cars which would be used out of the city or on non automated highways.

Other policies, in particular land use policy can also play an important role in the integration of public transport and land use, in ensuring that jobs and

128

housing opportunities are in balance, and in designing people friendly environments. If these objectives can be achieved, journey lengths would be reduced and the potential for using environmentally friendly modes (bus, cycle and walk) increased. Higher density mixed use developments in cities will enhance accessibility. It is in the suburbs that the increasing level of congestion is greatest and the solutions seem less clear (Cervero, 1989). The suburb to suburb movements on circumferential routes are ideal for the car, but the road capacity is limited. In the USA, congestion within the city is followed by similar levels of congestion in the suburbs and beyond.

It has taken over seventy years for the theory of road pricing (Pigou, 1920) to be matched with the technological requirements, and it may be many years before the political and social obstacles are overcome. Long before implementation takes place, the function and structure of cities may have changes, perhaps negating the need for road pricing in urban areas. It will be on the interurban routes where congestion will be endemic. Since 1985, 33 of the 239 head offices of the top 500 UK companies have moved head offices out of London, and this decentralisation has had a multiplier effect on support industries. Relocation is one obvious response to congestion. The question is whether road pricing would help to maintain London's position as a world city.

6. LINKS BETWEEN CHARGING AND FINANCING

One of the main unresolved issues concerning charging for the urban infrastructure is the use to be made of the substantial revenues which will be raised. In most European countries roads are built by governments and financed out of budgetary resources. Infrastructures are regarded as a collective public asset and their maintenance and construction are provided for from general tax revenue, although taxes are levied on transport (fuels and duty). Indirect taxes account for between 3 and 6 per cent of total government receipts (1.2-1.4 per cent of GDP), and as a rule income raised exceeds the total infrastructure expenditure by 25 per cent and this figure is increasing (European Parliament, 1991, p. 15).

The substantial public opposition to road pricing is reduced if the revenues are used to finance improvements in the road infrastructure and public transport. If the revenues are a means to raise additional tax revenue for the government, then the opposition is likely to be substantial (Chapter 5.2. Public Acceptance). Even if the revenues raised from road pricing are used for transport related investments, it should not be at the expense of other transport expenditure. The net effect should be a substantial increase in the levels of investment in the transport infrastructure. In addition, it is important that the new forms of road pricing are fiscally neutral, with the transference of the increased costs of travel by car onto the time and location of use, and a commensurate reduction in the existing costs of travel. Otherwise the net effects will be inflationary or result in major (unacceptable) changes in household expenditure patterns (Chapter 5.1. Equity).

Investment in the transport infrastructure is urgently needed and the debate has centred on the role that the private sector might have in the construction, maintenance and development of existing or new infrastructure, either on its own or in partnership with the public sector. The most attractive opportunities are on toll roads for the interurban road network, but there may also be limited opportunities for urban roads. In urban areas, the responsibilities for construction and maintenance are split between several different authorities, the statutory processes for construction of new roads are time consuming, and at present new road construction in urban areas is unlikely because of the high costs and public opposition. A greater opportunity lies in the management of the existing system through area traffic control systems, the use of the new Road Transport Informatics technology, and through the control of car parking (Chapter 4.1.). The private sector can be encouraged to organise and run these services, either for payment, or for a share of revenues from the charging systems. The private sector might also find such a role attractive as an opportunity to market some of their own hardware and software -- for dealing with congestion, vehicle security, vehicle location, traffic management and information exchange. The total world potential for RTI systems is estimated to grow to £27 billion by 2010 (NEDC, 1991).

All of these questions leave a feeling of uncertainty as to the way forward, in terms of the most appropriate strategy, the role of pricing, the role of the private sector, and the means by which implementation can take place. Clarification is certainly needed on the objectives of the charging system, so that the most appropriate system can be introduced and so that the public has a clear explanation of the rationale (see Table 6).

Road pricing and other forms of charging must be seen as part of a package of transport policy proposals, and also as part of a strategy for the city. Jones (1989, 1991) has identified a range of effective transport measures to restrict the use of the car which have been used in several European countries. These include:

-- Public transport improvements (service enhancements and/or fare reductions) as an integral part of any restraint packages on the car.
-- Where restraint policies have been successfully introduced, it has been for environmental reasons rather than alleviation of congestion (e.g. restraint on cars in central Athens and restrictions in several Italian cities). Environmental, energy, and safety considerations have been primary motives for lowering speed limits, not increasing road capacity.
-- A direct link between the revenues generated from road charges and the funding of transport and environmental improvements (e.g. the introduction of toll rings in Bergen and Oslo coincided with the opening of new sections of road).
-- Controversial schemes may first be proposed and introduced in smaller cities where the problems of implementation and any political implications are limited (e.g. the testing of the feasibility of the Norwegian toll ring concept in Bergen).
-- Support for restraint schemes has often increased after their introduction, once drivers have become used to them, and the benefits of reduced traffic levels are appreciated.

In addition to these transport considerations and the necessary preparation of the public for major change, the wider implications for the city as a whole need to be considered. These include:

-- Overcoming the perceived problems of competitive disadvantage of being the first city to introduced road pricing.
-- Identifying the most appropriate area for the implementation of the road pricing scheme. Evidence seems to be mixed as to whether the scheme in London should be restricted to the Central area (IPPR, 1989) or extend to the whole of the London area within the M25 (Chartered Institute of Transport, 1992). Boundary effects are likely to be considerable, particularly if the charged area is small.
-- Impacts on rent levels, land values, employment trends, labour turnover levels and the general local economic impact all need to be monitored. The London labour market and housing in London are both expensive, and additional travel costs may result in disadvantaging London's economy.
-- The distributional and equity questions need to be considered more thoroughly alongside the aggregate economic benefits. The evidence available is limited, and the impact on all household budgets is likely to be substantial. Road pricing will not just affect the lower income car owners, but all car owners. Payment of the proposed charges will increase average motoring budgets in car owning households by

40 per cent, so the impact on middle income households is also likely to be substantial.

-- Public acceptance of road pricing is still distant. They seem to understand the concept, but are totally against the imposition of an additional tax to bring their cars into the city centres, particularly if the revenue raised is for the exchequer. Congestion alleviation arguments do not seem to be convincing: the public is paying a charge for no guaranteed product. Even if environmental arguments are used, the case needs clarification as car drivers may simply switch to alternative destinations increasing journey lengths and fuel consumption.

In urban areas both the transport related and the broader planning arguments would argue against road pricing as car restraint policy. It could only be introduced in a clearly defined area as a limited part of a comprehensive policy which would have to have public acceptance.

7. PROMOTING POLICY ACTION

Gridlock is not only apparent on the roads, it is also part of institutional thinking. Radical alternatives are required. Transport systems management was used in the 1970s to increase the capacity of the road transport network through low cost schemes such as area traffic control, restrictions on parking, and extensive one way systems. This was followed by demand management in the 1980s to promote car sharing, new public transport systems, parking controls and pricing, and extensive pedestrianisation and calming schemes. In the 1990s, the options are reduced as the technological problems have been solved but there is an institutional reluctance to implement a road pricing policy or to use planning policy to limit the growth in traffic at source.

The question of public acceptability seems not to have been tested in Britain. There is an awareness of the problems caused by congestion, on the economy through wasted time and resources, on the environment through levels of pollution, and on the health of individuals through increased stress and frustration. Yet no government or local authority seems to be prepared to tackle the problem, either in terms of primary legislation which would be required to introduce road pricing (e.g. a requirement for vehicles to be fitted with a metering unit and for the right to charge for the use of the road), or using the already considerable development control and planning gain powers available to local authorities. The possibility of hypothecation of revenues raised from road pricing has not been

132

fully debated. The use of a substantial part of these monies for public transport improvements is necessary if public support is to be obtained. There is a fear of public reaction and a competitive disadvantage if only one city made such a decision.

The bus is the most efficient user of city road space, yet it has to share road space and this in turn reduces its efficiency. The urban road network could be designated for particular users. For example, in the city centre, 30 per cent of roads would be allocated to pedestrians and cyclists, a further 30 per cent to public transport and access only, and the remaining 40 per cent to general use. The proportions would not be uniform across the whole city but would relate to dominant land uses. A central shopping area might have a higher pedestrian allocation, whilst a peripheral office location might have only a limited pedestrian and public transport allocation, and a higher general allocation. The implementation of such a scheme could take place immediately, and the capacity of the bus system would be dramatically increased as scheduled operating speeds would be improved. There would be less cars in the city centre and the environmental benefits would also be significant. The real value of such a scheme would only materialise if a network of bus only routes is introduced and buses are completely separated from cars on "Green Routes". The "Red Routes" in London are a partial step to such a position as parking prohibitions are strictly enforced, allowing the free flow of traffic. But buses have to share road space with other traffic. Ironically, this option is now being considered in London in the context of bus deregulation as a set of exclusive rights of way would probably encourage greater on-street competition between operators. At present, unreliability costs operators over £100 million per annum in London through extra costs and lost revenue. In addition, the loss in travel time is significant, amounting to £127 million per annum in London.

Even in Cambridge, which may be the first British city to introduce road pricing, there is considerable emphasis on the fact that a trial will test the technical feasibility and the public acceptability of the scheme. Road pricing is only one part of the Cambridge strategy which also includes LRT (now replaced by a guided busway system), a Southern relief road, bus lanes, junction improvements, pedestrianisation, cycle schemes, a parking tow away scheme and a major new car park. These are all components of the integrated strategy and it will be interesting to see whether the strategy will eventually be implemented in its entirety or only in part (Hughes and Ison, 1992). Two points need to be made. The success of the strategy in Cambridge depends on the whole package being introduced, but it seems that most of the package will be introduced without the road pricing. If the road pricing is not included along with the other proposals, it is unlikely ever to be introduced. Secondly, it is advisable to introduce road pricing in a phased manner through raising parking charges and introducing cordon pricing prior to full implementation, probably at a zero charge to the user (at least initially). This would allow the public to get used to the concept of congestion pricing.

In other countries the problems of public acceptability has been tested through a referendum. Zurich, California and most recently Amsterdam have all used this means to assess whether political action would be supported by the electorate. California has taken the lead in imposing strict environmental limitations on car emissions, in encouraging zero emission vehicles, in using land use designations to reduce levels of trip generations, and in investment in public transport. Most emphasis has been placed on the journey to work problem and employers are seen as having a clear role to play in reducing trip rates. It is ironic that many of the radical proposals are being tested in the USA where the car culture is most dominant. These demonstration effects may also be important in arguing the case for applying charging systems more generally.

Road pricing has been described as the most successful theoretical but the least acceptable political contribution of economists to transport planning. This telling comment may have to be rewritten if public attitudes change, but the Harris Report gives little indication that the public is ready or even realise the full implications of ERP. At present, the political positions are in flux with the Conservatives reconsidering their position against road pricing, the Labour party is in favour of road pricing in principle, and the Liberal Democrats are in favour of supplementary licensing. Even if the political consensus is positive, implementation and reaction to the real situation is the acid test. A necessary prerequisite must be investment in public transport before pricing is introduced to reduce the painful transition and to have the capacity available. Perhaps a staged approach is required where car parking charges are raised substantially, then supplementary licensing is introduced, and finally road pricing.

The overriding question is whether road pricing in urban areas is required, and if so under what conditions. It is not a panacea. The functions of cities are changing, as are work patterns and other activities, and within the next ten years cities may no longer be suffering from road congestion. In the short term, it would be more appropriate to use restraint measures that are already available and accepted by the public -- land use controls, enforceable parking pricing and control strategies and the promotion of public transport, park and ride, cycling. Marginal cost pricing does not seem to be used in any other sector of the economy, so why should transport be identified as a special case. Unless all of these issues are fully researched and debated, road pricing may only hasten the death of the city rather than promote new life.

TABLES

Table 1. **Five options to combat congestion**

1. **Increase the amount of available road space:**
   * build more roads -- not likely to be supported in urban areas on a large scale, but only in specific locations.

2. **Use existing road space more effectively:**
   * traffic management -- delays can be reduced by 13 per cent by Microprocessor Optimised Vehicle Activators (MOVA) which controls the length of green times at vehicle activated signals;
   * better information -- use of real time information and variable message signs;
   * route guidance -- better static signposting, variable message signs, parking guidance and in vehicle units. In Cologne, up to 40 per cent of congestion is due to searching for parking spaces and route guidance can reduce travel times by 10 per cent;
   * matching demand and supply -- tidal flow operations, ramp metering and speeds -- as with 50 mph speed limits at peak times on parts of the M25 round London;
   * red routes -- strict enforcement of parking controls to allow free flow of traffic on main routes. In London there will be 500 km of red routes which can reduce travel times by up to 30 per cent between peaks and increase bus reliability by 40 per cent;
   * reducing illegal parking -- through heavy and enforceable fines, wheel clamping and the towing away of illegally parked vehicles. Some 70 000 vehicles are illegally parked in Central London every day and some 7 000 fixed penalty notices are issued each day: about ten per cent of offenders are caught;
   * lane priorities -- to encourage high occupancy vehicles.

3. **Shifting demand to other modes:**
   * pedestrianisation -- needs to be combined with availability of local facilities;
   * cycling -- networks of cycle routes required;
   * public transport -- in particular them encouragement of multimodal movement, including interchange facilities and park an ride: "seamless" public transport is required.

4. **Implementing non transport policies:**
   * changing patterns of activities -- including flexible work practices;
   * land use strategies and mixed development -- to minimise travel distances;
   * telecommuting -- potential for 15 per cent of all working by 1995.

5. **Restraining demand for car use:**
   * physical restraint -- traffic calming, parking restraints (in particular controls over private non residential parking: some 60 per cent of all parking spaces in Central London) and access restrictions (permits or licence plates);
   * increase the costs of using the car through real petrol price increases and through switching fixed costs to use costs;
   * road pricing;
   * parking control and pricing.

Source: Based on Institution of Highways and Transportation (1992) and other sources.

Table 2. **Methods of charging**

1. Off-Vehicle	Each vehicle has an identification number which is read by sensors at various points in the network. Charging is based on the number of points passed or the time spent between sensors. Used in the Hong Kong Electronic Road Pricing Demonstration.
2. On-Vehicle	Charges are related to the time spent within the designated area. New systems are much more flexible and changes can relate to traffic conditions, location and pollution levels. Payment can be made through a debit account or through a rechargeable card. Proposed in Cambridge and Richmond.
3. Manual System	Charges are collected on site or permits are purchased in advance and displayed in the vehicle. In Singapore, this system is used, but only for vehicles entering the city centre. Similar systems can be used to charge for parking.
4. Vehicle Excise Duty and Fuel Duty	Charges are collected annually and related to type of vehicle, capacity of vehicle and distance travelled. This form of charging is extensively used at present but could be further refined to relate to distance travelled. It is already used in a simple form in the freight sector as well as the passenger sector.

Table 3. **The arguments for road freight pricing**

1.	Transport costs are small in relation to final products costs, and equity problems are less than those in the passenger sector.
2.	There are fewer vehicles to be fitted if any special weight or distance or electronic device is needed.
3.	These vehicles should be operated in a more controlled environment than cars via the national quality licensing laws.
4.	Competition in the road freight sector is considerably distorted, for example through different safety standards on rail and road, but also between vehicles of different sizes.
5.	Road freight can be highly competitive, but extremely inefficient.
6.	Social and environmental costs which are not represented in the transport market, such as noise, vibration, pollution, fatal accidents and severance are far higher for heavy lorries than cars.

Source: Based on Buchan (1992).

Table 4. **Alternative strategies of households to meet road pricing charges**

1.	Switch mode from car to public transport: less car travel.
2.	Use public transport budget for car travel: less public transport travel.
3.	Increase proportion of household expenditure on transport: cutbacks in other items of household expenditure.
4.	Increase the household budget: inflationary if productivity is not also improved.
5.	Companies or a third party to pay charge: becomes a transfer payment and is ineffective.
6.	Switch within the car mode to another destination, route, time of day: increase flexibility in trip making to avoid charges.
7.	Suppress trip.

Table 5. **Central London charges at peak times**

Per cent of Respondents	Charges per hour whilst actually driving			
	50p	£1	£2	£5
Pay to use car in peak	73	63	45	23
Switch to public transport	14	20	34	51
Use car, but off peak	10	12	11	16
Not make journey at all	3	3	9	9

Table 6. **Relationships between road pricing objectives and the type of scheme introduced**

1. If the objective is to **reduce congestion** so that the external costs of transport can be internalised and road space is efficiently used (as in the United Kingdom), then:

   * a cordon, area licence, or travel-related charge may be appropriate, depending on the circumstances;
   * it will usually be desirable to locate the restricted area boundary at a point where traffic can detour to avoid payment, but the boundary should incorporate the main congested area;
   * charges are normally varied by time of day, being greatest at the peak and zero when traffic is light.

2. If the objective is to **raise revenue** for road building (as in Norway), then the maximum number of people should pay the minimum charge to deter trip suppression:

   * a cordon round the area is preferable, with little opportunity to detour or avoid the charge;
   * the cordon should be located to intercept the maximum number of trips;
   * the charge should be a uniform one, throughout the week, or for as long as is politically acceptable.

3. If the objective is an **environmental** one (the polluter pays principle), relating to the traffic pollution in an area, then:

   * charges may be lower for "green" vehicles;
   * an area-wide scheme (multiple cordons or an area licence) would be most appropriate;
   * the area covered would probably be larger than for traffic congestion objective;
   * there would probably be less time of day variation in price than with a congestion objective.

Source: Based on Jones (1990).

BIBLIOGRAPHY

Adams, J. (1989), Road Pricing for London, Mimeo, Department of Geography, University College London.

Association of County Councils (1991), Towards a Sustainable Transport Policy, Paper prepared by the Association of County Councils, November.

Banister, D. (1989), (ed.) The Final Gridlock, *Built Environment* 15 (3/4), pp. 159-256.

Banister, D. (1992a), The Congestion Gap: Planning and Technical Solutions, Paper presented at the Cambridge Econometrics Annual Conference on Transport, Communications and the Economy: Imagining the 21st Century, Cambridge, July.

Banister, D. (1992b), Energy use, transport and settlement patterns, in Breheny, M. (ed.), *Sustainable Development and Urban Form*, London: Pion, pp. 160-181.

Banister, D. and Mackett, R. (1990), The minibus: Theory and experience, and their Implications, *Transport Reviews* 10(3), pp. 189-241.

Bayliss, D. (1992), British views on road pricing, *Chartered Institute of Transport Proceedings* 1(4), pp. 3-13.

Buchan, K. (1992), The Congestion Gap: Market Based Investment Solutions, Paper presented at the Cambridge Econometrics Annual Conference on Transport, Communications and the Economy: Imagining the 21st Century, Cambridge, July.

Cervero, R. (1989), America's Suburban Centers: The Land-Use Transportation Link, Boston: Unwin Hyman.

Cervero, R. and Hall, P. (1989), Containing traffic congestion in America, *Built Environment* 15 (3/4), pp. 176-184.

Chartered Institute of Transport (1992), Paying for Progress, a Report on Congestion and Road Use Charges, *Supplementary Report*, London, March.

Commission of the European Communities (1990), Green Paper on The Urban Environment, Brussels, EUR 12902.

Commission of the European Communities (1991), The DRIVE Programme in 1991, DGXIII -- Telecommunications, Information Industries and Innovation, DR1202, Brussels, April.

Commission of the European Communities (1992), Future Development of the Common Transport Policy: A Global Approach to the Construction of a Community Framework for Sustainable Development, White Paper on Transport Policy, Com (92) 494, December, Brussels.

Confederation of British Industry (1992), London Transport Task Force Interim Report, Report by the CBI London Region Task Force, London, December.

Department of Transport (1993), London Congestion Charging, London, HMSO, March.

Evans, A.W. (1992), Road congestion pricing: When is it a good policy? *Journal of Transport Economics and Policy* 26(3), pp. 213-243.

European Parliament (1991), Community Policy on Transport Infrastructures, Research and Documentation Papers on Regional Policy and Transport, No. 16, EN-3-1991, Brussels.

Glazer, A. and Niskanen, E. (1992), Parking Fees and Congestion, *Regional Science and Urban Economics* 22(2), pp. 123-132.

Goldstein, A. (1989), Travel in London: Is Chaos Inevitable? The London Regional Transport sponsored lecture, November, p. 31.

Goodwin, P. and Jones, P. (1989), Road Pricing: The Political and Strategic Possibilities, ECMT Round Table 80: Systems of road infrastructure cost coverage, Paris, pp. 5-59.

Government Statistical Survey (1992), Family Expenditure Survey 1992, London, HMSO.

Group Transport 2000 Plus (1990), Transport in a Fast Changing Europe, Report produced by the Group set up by Karel Van Miert, Transport Commissioner of the European Commission, December.

Hughes, G. and Ison, S. (1992), The Cambridge congestion metering scheme, *Transport* 13(3), May-June, pp. 7-9.

Institute for Public Policy Research (1989), A Cleaner, Faster London: Road Pricing, Transport Policy and the Environment, London, IPPR.

Institution of Highways and Transportation (1992), Traffic Congestion in Urban Areas, A second position Paper on Current Policy Issues, IHT, September.

Jones, P. (1989), The restraint of road traffic in urban areas: Objectives, options and experiences, Rees Jeffrey's Discussion Paper 3, Transport Studies Unit, Oxford.

Jones, P. (1990), The road pricing debate in Europe, Mimeo, Transport Studies Group, Oxford, p. 9.

Jones, P. (1991), UK Public Attitudes to Urban Traffic Problems and Possible Countermeasures: A Poll of Polls, *Environment and Planning* C 9(3), pp. 245-258.

Jones, P. (1992), Review of Available Evidence on Public Reactions to Road Pricing, Report to the Department of Transport, July, p. 131.

Jones, P. (1993), Tackling Traffic Congestion: Facing up to the Realities, Inaugural Professorial Lecture, University of Westminster, March, p. 14.

Kashima, S. (1989), Advanced traffic information systems in Tokyo, *Built Environment* 15(3/4), pp. 244-250.

Knight, F.H. (1924), Some fallacies in the interpretation of social cost, *Quarterly Journal of Economics* 38, pp. 582-606.

Lex Motoring (1992), Lex Report on Motoring 1992, Report produced by MORI for Lex Motoring, London, January.

London Boroughs Association (1990), Road Pricing for London, Published by the LBA, 23 Buckingham Gate, London, May.

Marshall, A. (1890), *Principles of Economics*, London, Macmillan.

Ministry of Transport (1964), Road Pricing: The Economic and Technical Possibilities (the Smeed Report), London, HMSO.

National Economic Development Council (1991), Amber Alert: Relieving Urban Traffic Congestion, Report of the Traffic Management Systems Working Party, Chaired by John Ashworth.

National Economic Development Office (1991), A Road User Charge? Londoners' Views, Report prepared by the Harris Research Centre for NEDO, the London Planning Advisory Committee and the Automobile Association, London.

Pigou, A.C. (1920), *Wealth and Welfare*, London, Macmillan.

Small, K. (1992), *Urban Transportation Economics*, Fundamentals of Pure and Applied Economics, No. 51, Harwood, USA.

Tolley, R. (1990), *Calming Traffic in Residential Areas*, Tregaron: Brefi Press.

Verhoef, E., Nijkamp, P. and Rietveld, P. (1993), The Economics of Parking Management Systems: The (im)possibilities of parking policies in traffic regulation, Paper presented at the ETC European Transport Colloquium, Brussels, March.

Vogel, S. and Rowlands, I. (1990), The challenges and opportunities facing the European electronics information industry, in Locksley, G. (ed.), *The Single European Market and the Information and Communication Technologies*, London, Belhaven.

ANNEXES

ANNEX 1. Households' weekly expenditure on transport
-- from the Family Expenditure Survey (1991)

Gross income (£ per week)	Motoring (£)	Net purchase of vehicles, spares and accessories (£)	Maintenance and running costs (£)	Public transport fares and other costs (£)	Total expenditure on transport (£)	Total household expenditure (£)	Percentage of households with at least one car or van
< £60	1.76	0.54	1.22	1.54	3.30	62.97	8.5
£60-£80	2.64	0.57	2.07	1.57	4.21	79.08	15.3
£80-£100	4.37	1.14	3.23	1.93	6.30	105.90	23.1
£100-£125	5.99	1.73	4.26	2.50	8.49	122.70	30.3
£125-£150	13.91	5.97	7.94	2.26	16.17	146.80	45.7
£150-£175	11.79	4.10	7.69	2.91	14.70	160.76	51.6
£175-£225	21.89	10.13	11.76	3.60	25.49	194.73	65.9
£225-£275	24.41	10.06	14.35	4.69	29.10	221.42	72.7
£275-£325	30.16	12.32	17.85	4.53	34.69	243.16	80.8
£325-£375	37.15	17.52	19.63	5.88	43.03	272.04	84.3
£375-£425	45.72	25.03	20.68	5.84	51.56	299.84	88.5
£425-£475	43.33	20.06	23.27	5.72	49.05	300.51	90.1
£475-£550	58.14	33.10	25.04	8.06	66.20	358.25	93.6
£550-£650	65.16	35.51	29.65	7.70	72.86	396.07	95.7
£650-£800	72.44	37.48	34.95	11.10	83.54	442.89	97.5
> £800	80.44	43.93	36.51	15.76	96.20	586.93	97.6
TOTAL	34.12	17.08	17.04	5.58	39.70	259.04	67.8

The calculations in the text are based on the following assumptions:

(i) All the expenditure on motoring in each income category is spent in households with cars;

(ii) The average total household expenditure for car owning and non car owning households is the same;

(iii) The purpose of the analysis is to demonstrate the impacts of road pricing on household budgets assuming that five trips are made by each car owning household into the road pricing area each week.

ANNEX 1. Car owning households -- Expenditure patterns (1991)

Gross income (£ per week)	Expenditure on motoring (£ per week)	Percentage of average household budget	Percentage of average household budget with pricing
< £60	20.71	32.9	64.6
£60-£80	17.25	21.8	47.1
£80-£100	18.91	17.9	36.7
£100-£125	19.77	16.1	32.4
£125-£150	30.44	20.7	34.4
£150-£175	22.84	14.2	26.6
£175-£225	33.21	17.1	27.3
£225-£275	33.58	15.2	24.2
£275-£325	37.33	15.4	23.6
£325-£375	44.07	16.2	23.6
£375-£425	51.66	17.2	23.9
£425-£475	48.09	16.0	22.7
£475-£550	62.11	17.3	22.9
£550-£650	68.08	17.2	22.2
£650-£800	74.30	16.8	21.3
> £800	82.42	14.0	17.4
	50.32	19.4	27.1

ANNEX 2. Road Pricing in London

As much of the evidence quoted in this paper refers to the particular problems of congestion in London and as there is a current major project on Road Pricing in London, it is appropriate that a summary is presented as an annex.

1. **The London Road Pricing Study**: a three year programme of research which was started in May 1992 to investigate road pricing as a possible solution to congestion. The research is being co-ordinated by the MVA Consultancy.

---

1. Transport Modelling

A three tier structure has been established:
* Lower tier: detailed case study modelling of local traffic conditions.
* Middle tier: based on existing London Transportation Study model.
* Upper tier: new strategic model being developed by Marcial Echenique.

Inputs to the Model include:
* Choice of travel time (Oxford University, Accent, University of Westminster.
* Specification of model elasticities (Halcrow Fox, University of Leeds, Accent).
* Demand effects of travel time reliability (Cranfield Institute of Technology, Public Attitude Surveys).
* Reactions of commercial vehicles (John Fearon Consultancy, Touche Ross, Accent).
* Employer assistance (Transport Research Laboratory, Public Attitude Surveys, Price Waterhouse).

---

2. Public Attitudes

Research completed including public and business responses (University of Westminster, Accent).

---

3. Road Pricing Technology

Research completed (University of Newcastle, Intercai-ATS, London Research Centre).

---

4. Impact Assessment

Impact group assessment.
Environmental/safety assessment.

151

2.   From the Institute for Public Policy Research (1989, pp. 24-25):

In January 1989, the MVA Consultancy reported to the London Planning Advisory Committee the results of a desk study of road user charges, using the London Area Model (LAM) developed by the Transport and Road Research Laboratory to evaluate different systems of charges for moving vehicles within Central London. Removal of subsidies to company cars was included in each option tested.

The first option, Cordon Charging, would, as in Singapore, involve a supplementary charge for being in Central London during a weekday. Earlier studies suggested an optimum charge of £3 per day. On that basis, MVA estimated that weekday traffic terminating in Central London would be reduced by 30 per cent and through traffic by between 70-80 per cent. Demand for Central London buses would increase by 15 per cent and for trains/tubes by 7 per cent.

After allowing for the disbenefits to those diverted to other forms of travel, MVA estimated net benefits of around £140 million per annum, most of which would go to bus users, remaining car users -- those who "pay and stay" -- and other Central London road users, including delivery vehicles. In addition, the number of accidents would fall by some 4 per cent, and environmental damage, noise and pedestrian delay would be reduced significantly.

MVA also considered an Electronic Road Pricing option, allowing for a more complex and sensitive system than Cordon Charges. The ERP system which they tested divided Central London into 4 to 6 zones, with charges levied on entry to Central London and whenever a zonal boundary was crossed. As in the Hong Kong schemes, charges could be varied between peaks, interpeaks and the "shoulders" of the peaks, thus avoiding the problem of Cordon Charges which concentrate traffic just outside the charge period. MVA, however, tested a single charge of 70p for each charging point, on the basis that a typical two-way journey would cross two or three charging points in each direction. Thus, charges for a return journey would be between £2.80 and £4.20.

Drawing on the Hong Kong study, MVA estimated that ERP would produce benefits some 20 per cent higher than the Cordon Charging option with estimated net benefits of around £190 million per annum. Combining ERP with enhanced public transport (financed from ERP revenues) produced economic benefits of £310 million per annum. They concluded "the combination of ERP and enhanced public transport would produce substantial improvements in efficiency and accessibility and smaller improvements in the environment, safety, equity and economic activity".

A daily charge of £3 for driving in Central London would, according to the same model, increase traffic speeds for the remaining vehicles -- taxis, buses, delivery vehicles and other drivers who would "pay and stay" -- from below 13 miles per hour to between 16 and 19 miles per hour (an improvement of between 23 and 46 per cent).

3. Ministerial Statements on Road Pricing in London

1. Paul Channon, who set up a series of studies into the feasibility of road pricing in London, commented (June 1989) that it was "*a deeply unattractive prospect*".

2. Cecil Parkinson (6 December 1989) told the Commons Transport Select Committee "*there is no practical possibility of a London-wide road pricing scheme being introduced in any foreseeable time scale*".

3. Cecil Parkinson (11 June 1990) called the problem of introducing road pricing in London "*mind-boggling*". He criticised the concept on grounds of fairness, technology and enforcement, but did not rule out the "*possibility in the long term*".

4. Malcolm Rifkind (1991) set up the current major research programme on road pricing in London.

5. John MacGregor (31 March 1993) states that "*road pricing in London will be technologically feasible before the end of the century.*"

SUMMARY OF DISCUSSIONS

SUMMARY

1. THE EXISTING SITUATION

The proceedings of the Round Table began with the observation that whatever equilibrium there might at present be in the transport sector, in urban areas in particular, has had to be achieved despite time wasted in traffic snarls, wasted energy, pollution and a host of other disamenities. Faced with this situation, ordinary citizens and policymakers alike are increasingly concerned about restoring a modicum of wellbeing to city living -- and transport service quality is an ingredient in this process. There is a general desire to preserve what remains of each country's historical and natural heritage. Economic constraints being what they are, government authorities are seeking new sources of funding for transport infrastructure needs or offsetting public transport operating losses. A number of cities in this situation, but located in a variety of geographical areas, are investigating (if they have not already done so) the possibility of charging tolls on roads leading into their inner districts.

Urban road traffic congestion can have various explanations, ranging from chronic infrastructure inadequacy -- sometimes in a specific place -- to isolated or unforeseen incidents (such as accidents). As matters stand, the problem is a fundamental one that calls for solutions extending over the long term.

Among the possible solutions may be mentioned: increases in infrastructure capacity, traffic management based on new information technology (route guidance), switching demand to other modes (public transport, walking, cycling), land-use strategies, changing the pattern of infrastructure use.

Regarding the first of these ideas -- building new road space -- several Round Table specialists considered it impracticable, either because the cost of new urban infrastructure has become prohibitive or because new roads will attract greater demand, and this is no longer acceptable. It is not an approach that can continue to be envisaged, aside from absolutely necessary roadworks. Route guidance technologies show promise but, for the time being, all depends on the development of these technologies; the industrial effort required is such that nothing concrete in the way of applicable techniques has yet been decided upon.

159

Land-use strategy has a decisive influence on transport flows (volume, destinations, etc.). It is likewise a long-term process and one obviously that must not be neglected; however, it cannot provide a quick answer to infrastructure saturation problems. As to the development of alternatives to roads, and the use of roads, the introduction of urban road pricing in the form of tolls is a technique worth considering.

Urban toll systems can be both a way of raising revenues and a disincentive to highway use. They could in theory attain a twofold objective by helping to cover transport provision development costs and curbing excessive use of private cars. In practice, these two goals run into a maze of difficulties of all kinds, with the net result that city dwellers are often negatively disposed towards the idea of urban road tolls.

People tend to think of roads as a birthright freely available to all, unlike economists who hold that any good has, or should have, a price. The right to travel -- whether it is used to go to the workplace or for social relations -- is viewed as so fundamental that any monetary impediment to it arouses strong feelings. Drivers of private cars already feel they pay more than enough, perhaps because governments have not made the public sufficiently aware of the costs associated with private car use: road accidents, pollution, energy wastage, to mention but a few. Worse, the burden of an urban toll system would fall heavily on the most disadvantaged elements of the population, people who have no alternative to going to work by car, for example.

Urban tolls would not in any case curtail road use to any appreciable extent. Opinion polls and simulations have all found that high toll rates (e.g. £4 for entering London) would reduce road traffic by no more than 10 per cent at peak hours. Introducing urban tolls for reducing congestion and protecting the environment would at best only partially succeed; on the other hand, given the low elasticity of demand, it would bring in an impressive amount of money. The Round Table indeed demonstrated the central role accorded in any urban toll project to collecting and allocating the proceeds.

Unless the possibility exists of switching to other modes, people required to pay urban road tolls will object very energetically and end up decrying the whole of their area's transport policy. This is to say that the question of road pricing cannot be considered in isolation from the rest of a city's transport system.

Urban tolls would clearly have consequences for business, industry, services and shops. Employees could demand that any rise in personal transport budgets be paid for by their firm. This could produce a situation where road tolls would

160

no longer act as a deterrent to road use since the money spent on tolls would be offset by higher incomes. By driving up wage costs, it could even become an inflationary factor! Firms might also decide to move out of areas where tolls are in force. Some Round Table specialists took quite a different view, however. A drop in road use could, by reducing the time now lost to traffic congestion, improve transport productivity. It is certain that some people would definitely benefit from the introduction of a toll system.

Care would have to be taken that traffic congestion did not merely move away from one area to another where road tolls were not practised. If this were to occur, few of the hoped-for effects would be achieved.

None of the foregoing should be taken as ruling out the possibility of road tolls. What is important is to foresee their consequences. This means setting out clearly and exactly the objectives to be pursued and from there deciding on the transport policy measures needed to attain them.

Another aspect to be taken into consideration is the need to maintain the quality of public and private transport services which is now jeopardised by the spread of severe congestion. Tolls could provide the revenue needed in this context to develop public transport with a view to catering for mobility requirements over the longer term. It was in fact stressed during the Round Table that many private vehicle users have no public transport alternative owing to the all too familiar patterns of urban sprawl over considerable distances. Pricing the main access routes to city centres would therefore provide a by no means negligible source of revenue.

If drivers do not realise what is going on and are not told, they will see road pricing as just another form of taxation. It should also be noted that taxes on fuel can serve no other purpose than that of covering the cost of infrastructure development over the longer term because there is no differentiation of the tax paid according to time of day or particular area. Accordingly, this form of taxation is not a way of using "pricing" to achieve an optimal allocation of resources since, if it is to do that, the prices have to be transparent -- i.e. known in advance -- so as to curb the use of infrastructure. It can be seen that the latter aim is to some extent incompatible with a system of gearing the charges to traffic conditions in real time. The perfect road pricing system is therefore far from being established. The criteria to be applied for the regular users of the road involve a further inconsistency in that any discount offered would risk negating the deterrent effect of tolls and would favour those who can reasonably be assumed to have quite good incomes.

On several occasions, the Round Table specialists stressed the prohibitive costs of new urban roads. When effective road capacity is also factored into the analysis, it becomes clear that public transport is the better investment. With the exception of teleworking, which may reduce mobility, there is as yet no sign of a potential decline in mobility.

The essential aim of pricing is to restore freedom of choice to the individual, but it only works if other means of travel are available over the longer term: toll roads are therefore only part of the overall transport system and cannot be considered in isolation. In this context, real-time information on traffic conditions can certainly improve the capacity of the road network overall but, in the long run, will not be sufficient.

Some specialists pointed out that tolls would make users pay for unspecified improvements in transport and for indeterminate trip times, insofar as there might not be enough modal transfers to make a significant difference in the short-term, that is to say, before an attractive public transport alternative is provided.

With regard to the provision of public transport, the Round Table's verdict was that, where these services use toll roads, they too should pay a charge in the interests of equitable resource allocation. Given the number of passengers carried by public transport, the cost per head would in any case be low.

In eastern and central European countries, the use of the private car is regarded in a much more positive light than public transport, which is considered inefficient. These countries do, however, have the advantage of now being able to introduce a more rational approach to infrastructure use. It is also reasonable to assume that, if sound choices are made, the cost will be covered by users: the problem is to select the right priorities. One option might be to proceed in stages, for instance by setting tolls low at first. This could offer a way out of a situation in which people are unwilling to pay the "time" cost of transport yet, at the same time, are unable or unwilling to resign themselves to leaving the car behind.

The view of the Round Table specialists was that prices would have to reach high levels before people would be persuaded to abandon the car for good, the point at which we should see greater use of public transport, thus proportionately reducing the operating deficit that has to be covered. "Car pooling" would be more common, as would environmentally-friendly modes of transport such as cycling and walking.

2. FEASIBILITY OF URBAN TOLL SYSTEMS

The Round Table specialists stressed the fact that pricing could work as an incentive or a disincentive where the purchase or use of goods and services was concerned. It is a virtual necessity if available resources are to be properly allocated over the long term. In places where demand is strong, the levying of tolls provides funds which can be used to expand needed infrastructure in those places. Given the present situation, however -- and as was pointed out earlier in this summary --, forms of infrastructure other than roads could be developed.

The introduction of variable prices for use (reflecting peak hours, congested areas, etc.) could, as far as some of the demand is concerned, have a regulatory effect in the medium term. Improved automatic payment technology has made it easier to gear prices to traffic conditions.

Certain specialists warned against extending market economy principles to the whole of the transport sector. Consumers have a more restricted range of choice as regards transport than they do on the conventional goods market. The specialists nevertheless admitted that prices could play a role in the allocation of resources. Furthermore, the necessary allocation of costs among the agents involved in mobility helps to make the responsibilities and induced economic effects more transparent.

Other matters which must be considered are the timing and impacts of introducing a pricing system. Some of these impacts will have to be cushioned. An urban toll system must form part of a city's overall transport policy, and this policy in turn should provide alternatives in the shape of public transport for the least advantaged, charges for parking (a very effective deterrent to private car use), goal-oriented land-use planning, etc.

A number of these points were touched upon in the first part of this summary; the practicalities of introducing urban tolls will now be discussed.

The experience of a number of countries shows that, in order to gain public acceptance, the following sequence of steps is called for:

-- clear identification of the problems to be solved;
-- determination of the corresponding goals;
-- choice of solutions.

The whole operation should be fully transparent; no measure should give the impression of being "technocratically" imposed.

Round Table participants were also interested by the idea of, or rather the need for, lower fixed vehicle taxes in compensation. Such taxes do not in any case curb private car use. More generally, the Round Table specialists were of the opinion that all road taxes, including fuel taxes, should go towards covering the long-term costs of road use and highway development.

The specialists frequently came back to the question of the way in which toll proceeds should be spent. There again, it is known from experience that public acceptance of tolls depends among other things on the money collected being reinvested in transport. In the longer run, it is fair to surmise that central government will try to merge toll proceeds into the general budget; but diverting toll moneys is more difficult to justify if a clear statement of the uses to which proceeds will be put is one of the arguments advanced to persuade the public to accept the toll system. At a more political level, it is often a municipal authority's role to decide how to use funds collected from its own inhabitants, especially in the absence of the sort of standard organisational plan for all cities which a central government might wish to impose.

Certain Round Table specialists noted that permanently high tolls would encourage users to buy more economical vehicles, so levels of car use would be maintained. The logical extension of this view is that variable pricing does not always achieve the desired objectives. On the contrary, it is generally acknowledged for example that, despite high collection, checking and operating costs, the road tax disc system has led to no reduction in the use of private cars.

Parking restrictions (number of spaces, time, price) have likewise had only a limited effect if introduced on their own, but this is not the case if they are part of a package of measures which include tolls. It is essential to establish a coherent system.

The question of the redistributive effect of road pricing for users in different income groups was raised several times. Although, taken collectively, it appears to have a positive effect on the allocation of resources, this is not so on an individual level. Some way of compensating lower income groups should therefore be found. Clearly, the introduction of road pricing might well call for a re-appraisal of the entire personal taxation system. Another obstacle is the fact that road users have learned to live with the inconveniences of congestion -- except its external effects -- and so are not keen on paying to eliminate a problem which they have, to all intents and purposes, accepted.

Toll systems can be considered to have three objectives: to raise extra revenue, reduce congestion and improve the environment. The evidence shows that the optimal price level differs for each of these objectives when taken on its own. It is therefore essential to define goals clearly and to keep a close eye on the results over the course of time. The cost of disrupting the status quo has to be borne in mind. It is also reasonable to say that tolls simply postpone the need to deal with the problem: the time costs are those generated by ever-increasing mobility.

With modern information and, more particularly, communications technologies, several specialists thought that it would be possible to introduce highly flexible pricing, varying with the route and the time of day. However, these are expensive systems and there might be opposition if they are not easily readable. Indeed, the more sophisticated the technology, the greater the need for careful presentation, clear explanation, training and preparatory work.

A number of specialists also thought that those who generate mobility, whether industry or services, should help to cover the costs. Moreover, if we are to find a lasting solution to our current mobility problems, at least some of the proceeds should be ploughed back into transport. Otherwise, the problem could prove to be self-perpetuating, with increasing saturation of infrastructure leading to higher and higher tolls, since marginal costs too would creep steadily upwards. A further point raised was that new roads attract greater demand.

From the foregoing it is clear that only a change of attitude will produce any real results. We are all equally responsible for congestion, every time we use the car when other alternatives are available but are overlooked or rejected.

From a more theoretical economic viewpoint, certain specialists took the view that tolls amount to more than a mere transfer of resources -- a zero-sum game, so to speak -- and that the whole community can benefit from the resulting gains in transport efficiency. This argument was, however, disputed by others who pointed to the regressive redistributive effect that tolls might produce.

This last consideration has particular relevance for the central and eastern European countries, where a huge appetite for private car use exists and scarcity of public resources could make tolls an almost inevitable solution while if past experience is any guide, severely hampering the development of public transport alternatives. The feeling of the Round Table was that these countries had the opportunity of introducing tolls as part of the sweeping changes they are undergoing. It is to be hoped that the West's mistakes -- which basically consist in discovering too late that prior choices have taken too little account of what have eventually turned out to be the real needs in the field of transport -- will not be repeated. It is indeed vital to foresee transport-related impacts in time.

Public transport operations are also deserving of consideration. Any new subsidies, or existing ones for that matter, must be subject to careful scrutiny as regards their use. This is an area where progress has been made, thanks to the standards of efficiency now required of public transport operators. The organisational solution applied in the United Kingdom, which consists in encouraging competition between carriers, has in fact produced results in terms of productivity. Lastly, the timeliness and cost of major public transport infrastructure investment need to be strictly evaluated, from the point of view of function and location, in a situation where cities are changing.

3. CONCLUSIONS

The difficulties associated with transport in urban areas, and the many consequences that stem from them, have reached a stage where they may be considered almost as a "problem of society", to use a much-abused phrase.

There are solid arguments for believing in the regulatory effects of pricing. If pricing instruments are to be used, however, their goals must, since they require changes in people's attitudes, be clearly stated; and complementary measures or policies must be introduced in conditions of complete transparency.

Where environmental impact is concerned, for example, significant progress can be expected from likely technological developments in vehicle design. These developments will be governed by national or international, not local, regulations, whereas tolls will be introduced at the local level. It is therefore at local level that the corresponding action will have to be taken.

In an urban context, compensatory measures will be essential. For tolls to work, prices will have to be high enough to bring about changes in attitudes -- more "car pooling", for instance, or significant modal shifts. It would therefore be not only fair but sensible to increase the provision of public transport, while ensuring that this alternative remains intrinsically competitive.

The Round Table participants considered that independent transport agencies could be given the task of organising all transport and of managing transport resources in each urban area. While such a step would almost certainly subject transport more directly to market forces, it would ensure full recognition of the specific character of the transport sector.

LIST OF PARTICIPANTS

Mrs Christiane DELEPIERE-DRAMAIS
Directeur de recherche
Groupe d'Économie des Transports
Institut de Sociologie
Université Libre de Bruxelles
Avenue Jeanne 44
B-1050 BRUXELLES

Chairman

Dr. David BANISTER
Bartlett School of Architecture and Planning
University College London
Wates House
22 Gordon Street
GB-LONDON WC1H 0QB

Rapporteur

Mr. Arild HERVIK
Møreforskningen
Postboks 308
N-6401 MOLDE

Rapporteur

Mr. Svein BRAATHEN
Møreforsking Molde
Postboks 406
N-6401 MOLDE

Co-Rapporteur

Mr. Heero D.P. POL
Ministry of Transport and Public Works
Directorate-General of Transport
P.O. box 20903
NL-2500 EX THE HAGUE

Rapporteur

Professor H. BAUER
Geschäftsführer
Kommunalwissenschaftliches Dokumentationszentrum (KDZ)
Mariahilferstrasse 136
A-1150 WIEN

Mr. David BAYLISS
Director of Planning
London Regional Transport
55 Broadway
GB-LONDON SW1H 0BD

Dr. F. BERNALDO DE QUIROS ROBLES
TEMA, Grupo Consultor, S.A.
Avenida de América 37 - Planta 1a
Torres Blancas
E-28002 MADRID

Mr. Michael BERTRAM
Project Manager
PROGNOS AG
Missionsstrasse 62
CH-4012 BASEL

Professor G.J. BLAUWENS
Universiteit Antwerpen (UFSIA)
Prinsstraat 13
B-2000 ANTWERPEN

Mr. G. EMMANOULOPOULOS
4 Papadiamantopoulou Str.
GR-11528 ATHENS

Professeur G. EVREN
Université Technique d'Istanbul (ITU)
Faculté du Génie Civil
Ayazaga Kampusu
TR-80626 AYAZAGA ISTANBUL

Mr. Brian FYNES
Transport Policy Research Institute
University College Dublin
Belfield
IRL-DUBLIN 4

Professor Peter J. HILLS
Director, Transport Operations Research Group
Civil Engineering Department
University of Newcastle upon Tyne
Claremont Tower
GB-NEWCASTLE UPON TYNE NE1 7RU

Mr. Simon HUIBERTS
Secretary, Technical Affairs
Nederlands Vervoer
P.O. Box 90417
NL-2509 LK THE HAGUE

Dr. Pierre-André JACCARD
Économiste
Institut des Transports et de Planification
ITEP, LEM
Ecole Polytechnique Fédérale de Lausanne
Ecublens - Génie Civil
CH-1015 LAUSANNE

171

Professor Peter JONES
Transport Studies Group
University of Westminster
35 Marylebone Road
GB-LONDON NW1 5LS

Mrs. Zsuzsa KAPITANY
Institute of Economics
Hungarian Academy of Sciences
Budaørsi u. 45
H-1112 BUDAPEST

Mr. André LAUER
Directeur du Centre d'Études
des Transports Urbains (CETUR)
Ministère de l'Équipement et du Logement
des Transports et de l'Espace
8 avenue Aristide Briand
F-92220 BAGNEUX

Professor Sulevi LYLY
Helsinki University of Technology
Laboratory of Transportation Engineering
Rakentajanaukio, 4 A
SF-02150 ESPOO

Mr. L. OLSSON
Göteborgsregionens Lokaltrafik AB
Box 405
S-401 26 GÖTEBORG

Professor Marco PONTI
c/o SISTAV-ITALFERR
Piazza Freud 1
I-2154 MILANO

Professor Francesc ROBUSTÉ
Universitat Politècnica de Catalunya
ETS Ingenieros de Caminos
Gran Capita S/N, Modul B1
E-08034 BARCELONA

Mr. Pierre-Yves TEXIER
Directeur du Département Analyse et
Régulation du Trafic (DART)
INRETS
B.P. 34
F-94114 ARCUEIL CEDEX

ECMT SECRETARIAT

Mr. Jack SHORT
Deputy Secretary-General

ECONOMIC RESEARCH AND DOCUMENTATION DIVISION

Mr. Arthur DE WAELE
Head of de Division

Mr. Michel VIOLLAND
Administrator

Ms Françoise ROULLET
Assistant

Ms Jane MINOUX
Assistant

Marketing and Service Quality in Public Transport. Series ECMT - Round Table 92 (1993)
(75 93 05 1) ISBN 92-821-1184-9   France FF150   Other Countries FF195   US$34 DM62

Benefits of Different Transport Modes. Series ECMT - Round Table 93 (1994)
(75 94 01 1) ISBN 92-821-1189-X   France FF80   Other Countries FF105   US$18 DM30

Regional Policy, Transport Networks and Communications. Series ECMT - Round Table 94
(1994)
(75 94 04 1) ISBN 92-821-1191-1   France FF100   Other Countries FF130   US$22 DM40

Transport Infrastructure and Systems for a New Europe. Series ECMT - Round Table 95
(1994)
(75 94 06 1) ISBN 92-821-1182-2   France FF110   Other Countries FF140   US$25 DM43

Short-distance Passenger Travel. Series ECMT - Round Table 96 (1994)
(75 94 09 1) ISBN 92-821-1193-8   France FF110   Other Countries FF145   US$27 DM43

Prices charged at the OECD Bookshop.

*The OECD CATALOGUE OF PUBLICATIONS and supplements will be sent free of charge
on request addressed either to OECD Publications Service,
or to the OECD Distributor in your country.*

MAIN SALES OUTLETS OF OECD PUBLICATIONS
PRINCIPAUX POINTS DE VENTE DES PUBLICATIONS DE L'OCDE

ARGENTINA – ARGENTINE
Carlos Hirsch S.R.L.
Galería Güemes, Florida 165, 4° Piso
1333 Buenos Aires   Tel. (1) 331.1787 y 331.2391
Telefax: (1) 331.1787

AUSTRALIA – AUSTRALIE
D.A. Information Services
648 Whitehorse Road, P.O.B 163
Mitcham, Victoria 3132   Tel. (03) 873.4411
Telefax: (03) 873.5679

AUSTRIA – AUTRICHE
Gerold & Co.
Graben 31
Wien I   Tel. (0222) 533.50.14

BELGIUM – BELGIQUE
Jean De Lannoy
Avenue du Roi 202
B-1060 Bruxelles   Tel. (02) 538.51.69/538.08.41
Telefax: (02) 538.08.41

CANADA
Renouf Publishing Company Ltd.
1294 Algoma Road
Ottawa, ON K1B 3W8   Tel. (613) 741.4333
Telefax: (613) 741.5439

Stores:
61 Sparks Street
Ottawa, ON K1P 5R1   Tel. (613) 238.8985
211 Yonge Street
Toronto, ON M5B 1M4   Tel. (416) 363.3171
Telefax: (416)363.59.63

Les Éditions La Liberté Inc.
3020 Chemin Sainte-Foy
Sainte-Foy, PQ G1X 3V6   Tel. (418) 658.3763
Telefax: (418) 658.3763

Federal Publications Inc.
165 University Avenue, Suite 701
Toronto, ON M5H 3B8   Tel. (416) 860.1611
Telefax: (416) 860.1608

Les Publications Fédérales
1185 Université
Montréal, QC H3B 3A7   Tel. (514) 954.1633
Telefax : (514) 954.1635

CHINA – CHINE
China National Publications Import
Export Corporation (CNPIEC)
16 Gongti E. Road, Chaoyang District
P.O. Box 88 or 50
Beijing 100704 PR   Tel. (01) 506.6688
Telefax: (01) 506.3101

DENMARK – DANEMARK
Munksgaard Book and Subscription Service
35, Nørre Søgade, P.O. Box 2148
DK-1016 København K   Tel. (33) 12.85.70
Telefax: (33) 12.93.87

FINLAND – FINLANDE
Akateeminen Kirjakauppa
Keskuskatu 1, P.O. Box 128
00100 Helsinki
Subscription Services/Agence d'abonnements :
P.O. Box 23
00371 Helsinki   Tel. (358 0) 12141
Telefax: (358 0) 121.4450

FRANCE
OECD/OCDE
Mail Orders/Commandes par correspondance:
2, rue André-Pascal
75775 Paris Cedex 16   Tel. (33-1) 45.24.82.00
Telefax: (33-1) 49.10.42.76
Telex: 640048 OCDE

OECD Bookshop/Librairie de l'OCDE :
33, rue Octave-Feuillet
75016 Paris   Tel. (33-1) 45.24.81.67
(33-1) 45.24.81.81

Documentation Française
29, quai Voltaire
75007 Paris   Tel. 40.15.70.00

Gibert Jeune (Droit-Économie)
6, place Saint-Michel
75006 Paris   Tel. 43.25.91.19

Librairie du Commerce International
10, avenue d'Iéna
75016 Paris   Tel. 40.73.34.60

Librairie Dunod
Université Paris-Dauphine
Place du Maréchal de Lattre de Tassigny
75016 Paris   Tel. (1) 44.05.40.13

Librairie Lavoisier
11, rue Lavoisier
75008 Paris   Tel. 42.65.39.95

Librairie L.G.D.J. - Montchrestien
20, rue Soufflot
75005 Paris   Tel. 46.33.89.85

Librairie des Sciences Politiques
30, rue Saint-Guillaume
75007 Paris   Tel. 45.48.36.02

P.U.F.
49, boulevard Saint-Michel
75005 Paris   Tel. 43.25.83.40

Librairie de l'Université
12a, rue Nazareth
13100 Aix-en-Provence   Tel. (16) 42.26.18.08

Documentation Française
165, rue Garibaldi
69003 Lyon   Tel. (16) 78.63.32.23

Librairie Decitre
29, place Bellecour
69002 Lyon   Tel. (16) 72.40.54.54

GERMANY – ALLEMAGNE
OECD Publications and Information Centre
August-Bebel-Allee 6
D-53175 Bonn   Tel. (0228) 959.120
Telefax: (0228) 959.12.17

GREECE – GRÈCE
Librairie Kauffmann
Mavrokordatou 9
106 78 Athens   Tel. (01) 32.55.321
Telefax: (01) 36.33.967

HONG-KONG
Swindon Book Co. Ltd.
13–15 Lock Road
Kowloon, Hong Kong   Tel. 366.80.31
Telefax: 739.49.75

HUNGARY – HONGRIE
Euro Info Service
Margitsziget, Európa Ház
1138 Budapest   Tel. (1) 111.62.16
Telefax : (1) 111.60.61

ICELAND – ISLANDE
Mál Mog Menning
Laugavegi 18, Pósthólf 392
121 Reykjavik   Tel. 162.35.23

INDIA – INDE
Oxford Book and Stationery Co.
Scindia House
New Delhi 110001   Tel.(11) 331.5896/5308
Telefax: (11) 332.5993
17 Park Street
Calcutta 700016   Tel. 240832

INDONESIA – INDONÉSIE
Pdii-Lipi
P.O. Box 269/JKSMG/88
Jakarta 12790   Tel. 583467
Telex: 62 875

ISRAEL
Praedicta
5 Shatner Street
P.O. Box 34030
Jerusalem 91430   Tel. (2) 52.84.90/1/2
Telefax: (2) 52.84.93

R.O.Y.
P.O. Box 13056
Tel Aviv 61130   Tél. (3) 49.61.08
Telefax (3) 544.60.39

ITALY – ITALIE
Libreria Commissionaria Sansoni
Via Duca di Calabria 1/1
50125 Firenze   Tel. (055) 64.54.15
Telefax: (055) 64.12.57

Via Bartolini 29
20155 Milano   Tel. (02) 36.50.83

Editrice e Libreria Herder
Piazza Montecitorio 120
00186 Roma   Tel. 679.46.28
Telefax: 678.47.51

Libreria Hoepli
Via Hoepli 5
20121 Milano   Tel. (02) 86.54.46
Telefax: (02) 805.28.86

Libreria Scientifica
Dott. Lucio de Biasio 'Aeiou'
Via Coronelli, 6
20146 Milano   Tel. (02) 48.95.45.52
Telefax: (02) 48.95.45.48

JAPAN – JAPON
OECD Publications and Information Centre
Landic Akasaka Building
2-3-4 Akasaka, Minato-ku
Tokyo 107   Tel. (81.3) 3586.2016
Telefax: (81.3) 3584.7929

KOREA – CORÉE
Kyobo Book Centre Co. Ltd.
P.O. Box 1658, Kwang Hwa Moon
Seoul   Tel. 730.78.91
Telefax: 735.00.30

MALAYSIA – MALAISIE
Co-operative Bookshop Ltd.
University of Malaya
P.O. Box 1127, Jalan Pantai Baru
59700 Kuala Lumpur
Malaysia   Tel. 756.5000/756.5425
Telefax: 757.3661

MEXICO – MEXIQUE
Revistas y Periodicos Internacionales S.A. de C.V.
Florencia 57 - 1004
Mexico, D.F. 06600   Tel. 207.81.00
Telefax : 208.39.79

NETHERLANDS – PAYS-BAS
SDU Uitgeverij Plantijnstraat
Externe Fondsen
Postbus 20014
2500 EA's-Gravenhage   Tel. (070) 37.89.880
Voor bestellingen: Telefax: (070) 34.75.778

NEW ZEALAND
NOUVELLE-ZÉLANDE
Legislation Services
P.O. Box 12418
Thorndon, Wellington   Tel. (04) 496.5652
Telefax: (04) 496.5698

NORWAY – NORVÈGE
Narvesen Info Center – NIC
Bertrand Narvesens vei 2
P.O. Box 6125 Etterstad
0602 Oslo 6 Tel. (022) 57.33.00
Telefax: (022) 68.19.01

PAKISTAN
Mirza Book Agency
65 Shahrah Quaid-E-Azam
Lahore 54000 Tel. (42) 353.601
Telefax: (42) 231.730

PHILIPPINE – PHILIPPINES
International Book Center
5th Floor, Filipinas Life Bldg.
Ayala Avenue
Metro Manila Tel. 81.96.76
Telex 23312 RHP PH

PORTUGAL
Livraria Portugal
Rua do Carmo 70-74
Apart. 2681
1200 Lisboa Tel.: (01) 347.49.82/5
Telefax: (01) 347.02.64

SINGAPORE – SINGAPOUR
Gower Asia Pacific Pte Ltd.
Golden Wheel Building
41, Kallang Pudding Road, No. 04-03
Singapore 1334 Tel. 741.5166
Telefax: 742.9356

SPAIN – ESPAGNE
Mundi-Prensa Libros S.A.
Castelló 37, Apartado 1223
Madrid 28001 Tel. (91) 431.33.99
Telefax: (91) 575.39.98

Librería Internacional AEDOS
Consejo de Ciento 391
08009 – Barcelona Tel. (93) 488.30.09
Telefax: (93) 487.76.59

Llibreria de la Generalitat
Palau Moja
Rambla dels Estudis, 118
08002 – Barcelona
(Subscripcions) Tel. (93) 318.80.12
(Publicacions) Tel. (93) 302.67.23
Telefax: (93) 412.18.54

SRI LANKA
Centre for Policy Research
c/o Colombo Agencies Ltd.
No. 300-304, Galle Road
Colombo 3 Tel. (1) 574240, 573551-2
Telefax: (1) 575394, 510711

SWEDEN – SUÈDE
Fritzes Information Center
Box 16356
Regeringsgatan 12
106 47 Stockholm Tel. (08) 690.90.90
Telefax: (08) 20.50.21

Subscription Agency/Agence d'abonnements :
Wennergren-Williams Info AB
P.O. Box 1305
171 25 Solna Tel. (08) 705.97.50
Téléfax : (08) 27.00.71

SWITZERLAND – SUISSE
Maditec S.A. (Books and Periodicals – Livres
et périodiques)
Chemin des Palettes 4
Case postale 266
1020 Renens Tel. (021) 635.08.65
Telefax: (021) 635.07.80

Librairie Payot S.A.
4, place Pépinet
CP 3212
1002 Lausanne Tel. (021) 341.33.48
Telefax: (021) 341.33.45

Librairie Unilivres
6, rue de Candolle
1205 Genève Tel. (022) 320.26.23
Telefax: (022) 329.73.18

Subscription Agency/Agence d'abonnements :
Dynapresse Marketing S.A.
38 avenue Vibert
1227 Carouge Tel.: (022) 308.07.89
Telefax : (022) 308.07.99

See also – Voir aussi :
OECD Publications and Information Centre
August-Bebel-Allee 6
D-53175 Bonn (Germany) Tel. (0228) 959.120
Telefax: (0228) 959.12.17

TAIWAN – FORMOSE
Good Faith Worldwide Int'l. Co. Ltd.
9th Floor, No. 118, Sec. 2
Chung Hsiao E. Road
Taipei Tel. (02) 391.7396/391.7397
Telefax: (02) 394.9176

THAILAND – THAÏLANDE
Suksit Siam Co. Ltd.
113, 115 Fuang Nakhon Rd.
Opp. Wat Rajbopith
Bangkok 10200 Tel. (662) 225.9531/2
Telefax: (662) 222.5188

TURKEY – TURQUIE
Kültür Yayinlari Is-Türk Ltd. Sti.
Atatürk Bulvari No. 191/Kat 13
Kavaklidere/Ankara Tel. 428.11.40 Ext. 2458
Dolmabahce Cad. No. 29
Besiktas/Istanbul Tel. 260.71.88
Telex: 43482B

UNITED KINGDOM – ROYAUME-UNI
HMSO
Gen. enquiries Tel. (071) 873 0011
Postal orders only:
P.O. Box 276, London SW8 5DT
Personal Callers HMSO Bookshop
49 High Holborn, London WC1V 6HB
Telefax: (071) 873 8200
Branches at: Belfast, Birmingham, Bristol, Edin-
burgh, Manchester

UNITED STATES – ÉTATS-UNIS
OECD Publications and Information Centre
2001 L Street N.W., Suite 700
Washington, D.C. 20036-4910 Tel. (202) 785.6323
Telefax: (202) 785.0350

VENEZUELA
Libreria del Este
Avda F. Miranda 52, Aptdo. 60337
Edificio Galipán
Caracas 106 Tel. 951.1705/951.2307/951.1297
Telegram: Libreste Caracas

Subscription to OECD periodicals may also be
placed through main subscription agencies.

Les abonnements aux publications périodiques de
l'OCDE peuvent être souscrits auprès des
principales agences d'abonnement.

Orders and inquiries from countries where Distribu-
tors have not yet been appointed should be sent to:
OECD Publications Service, 2 rue André-Pascal,
75775 Paris Cedex 16, France.

Les commandes provenant de pays où l'OCDE n'a
pas encore désigné de distributeur devraient être
adressées à : OCDE, Service des Publications,
2, rue André-Pascal, 75775 Paris Cedex 16, France.

9-1994

OECD PUBLICATIONS, 2 rue André-Pascal, 75775 PARIS CEDEX 16
PRINTED IN FRANCE
(75 94 11 1) ISBN 92-821-1195-6- No. 47537 1994

2960 002